insight text guide

Victoria Bladen

The Taming of the Shrew

William Shakespeare

First published in 2021, reprinted in 2023.

Insight Publications Pty Ltd
3/350 Charman Road
Cheltenham VIC 3192
Australia
Tel: +61 3 8571 4950
Fax: +61 3 8571 0257
Email: books@insightpublications.com.au

www.insightpublications.com.au

A catalogue record for this book is available from the National Library of Australia

William Shakespeare's The Taming of the Shrew / Victoria Bladen

Victoria Bladen asserts the moral right to be identified as the author of this work.

ISBNs:
9781922525529 (print)
9781922525536 (digital)
9781922525543 (bundle: print + digital)

Cover design by Gisela Beer

Printed by Markono Print Media Pte Ltd

For Ann and Kate, two wonderful shrews.

contents

Character map iv

Overview 1

About the author 2

Synopsis 3

Character summaries 6

Background & context 7

Genre, structure & language 11

Scene-by-scene analysis 16

Characters & relationships 40

Themes, ideas & values 47

Different interpretations 58

Questions & answers 63

Sample answer 72

References & reading 74

CHARACTER MAP

The Induction (frame narrative)

Hostess
argues with
Christopher Sly
tinker
plays a trick on
Lord
watches a play
performed by
pretends to
be wife of
page
Bartholomew
Troupe of actors
performs

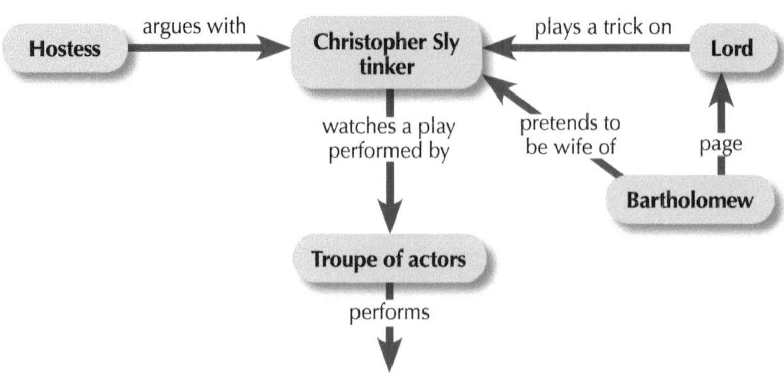

The Taming of the Shrew

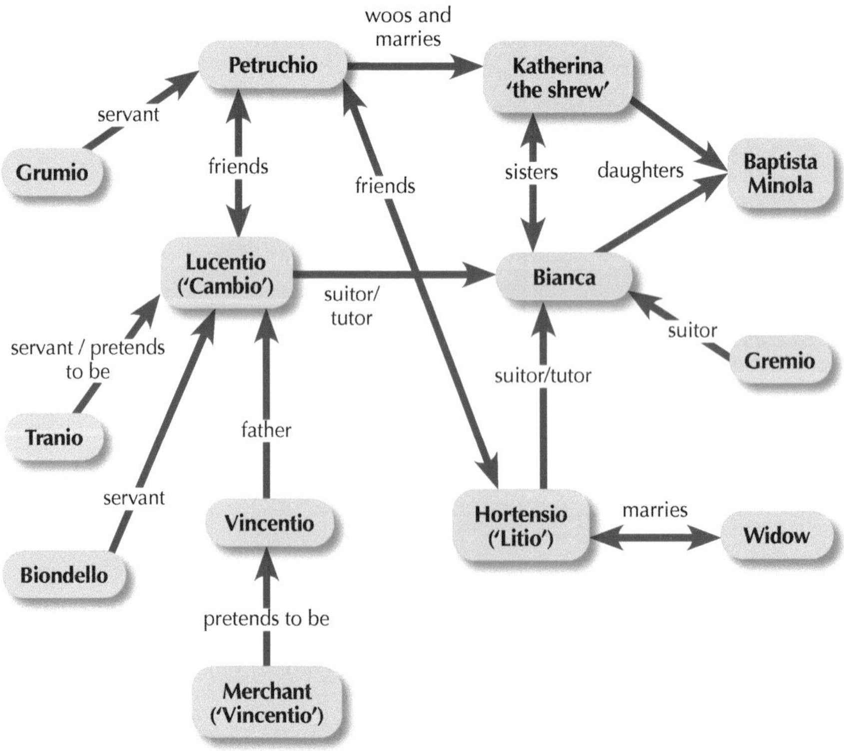

woos and
marries
Petruchio
Katherina
'the shrew'
servant
Grumio
friends
friends
sisters
daughters
Baptista
Minola
Lucentio
('Cambio')
suitor/
tutor
Bianca
suitor
Gremio
servant / pretends
to be
Tranio
father
suitor/tutor
servant
Vincentio
Hortensio
('Litio')
marries
Widow
Biondello
pretends to be
Merchant
('Vincentio')

OVERVIEW

William Shakespeare (1564–1616) is one of the most renowned figures of the English literary Renaissance (also referred to as the 'early modern period'). His dramatic and poetic work, written during an intensely productive period from the late sixteenth to the early seventeenth century, has proved capable of enduring well beyond his own time and place. Translated into many languages and adapted for film, television, ballet, opera and graphic novels, Shakespeare's work has evolved into a cultural phenomenon, meaningful and compelling to audiences of different eras and cultures.

The Taming of the Shrew, written around 1590–91 during the Elizabethan period, is one of Shakespeare's problematic comedies and raises important questions about gender relations and the treatment of women. *Shrew* is a difficult play for the contemporary stage, due to our increased awareness of gendered violence and the various forms that this can take: not only physical but verbal and psychological.

Remember that *The Taming of the Shrew* is a *play,* intended as a performance on stage, even though we often first experience it as a written text or film. If you are able to see the play performed, you will gain a deeper understanding of its shape, the characters, how the dramatic action unfolds and the effect of Shakespeare's language. Film adaptations will also help you to understand the play, particularly if you are able to view different versions. However, watching a film should not be a substitute for a close reading of the text itself.

About the author

Shakespeare was born in 1564, when Elizabeth I was on the throne, and died in 1616, when James I was king. Born into a middle-class family in Stratford-upon-Avon, in Warwickshire, William was the son of John Shakespeare, a glove-maker and landowner, and his wife Mary, a gentleman's daughter. Shakespeare received an education at the King's New School in Stratford, but never attended university. As a young man he fell in love with Anne Hathaway, and they were married in 1582 after Anne became pregnant; the child, Susanna, was born six months after the wedding. Twins, Hamnet and Judith, were born in 1585; Hamnet died as a child. Subsequently, the marriage appears to have broken down.

In the late 1580s, Shakespeare moved to London and began his career as a playwright. He joined a theatre company called the Lord Chamberlain's Men (also briefly known as Lord Hunsdon's Men), under the patronage of the Lord Chamberlain. The ensemble produced plays that were performed at a venue called the Theatre. Shakespeare acted in, wrote plays for and shared in the profits of the theatre company. When the lease over the land on which the Theatre was built expired in 1597 and a dispute with the landlord arose, Shakespeare and his colleagues dismantled the wooden building, took it across the river and reassembled it at Bankside, south of the Thames. This theatre, renamed the Globe, opened in 1599. In London today, a close replica of the Globe stands near the original site, and Shakespeare's plays are performed there all year round.

When James I came to the throne in 1603, he became the patron of the theatre company of which Shakespeare was part owner; the company was therefore renamed the King's Men. The King recognised the huge potential of the theatre to reach many people; in this regard, the theatre can perhaps be thought of as the early seventeenth-century equivalent of television or the internet. James wanted his reign to be associated with that 'media' power, despite the fact that in many of Shakespeare's works there is strong criticism of authority figures.

Synopsis

The Taming of the Shrew presents two stories of wooing. The main plot line centres on Katherina, an outspoken woman – a 'shrew' – who is wooed, and supposedly 'tamed' by Petruchio, an eccentric gentleman who has arrived in Padua in search of a wife and who likes a challenge. The subsidiary plot involves Katherina's sister Bianca, who conforms to the behaviour expected of women in this period and is pursued by various competing suitors young and old. A further story envelops these, serving as a frame narrative that creates a play-within-a-play.

Before the first act of the main play begins, the frame narrative is established with a two-part Induction scene. A drunken tinker, Sly, after an argument with a hostess, passes out outside an alehouse. A Lord, returning from hunting, decides to play a trick on him and, upon Sly waking from his drunken stupor, the Lord and his attendants pretend that Sly is a wealthy lord who suffered temporary insanity, thus believing himself to be a lowborn tinker. The Lord's attendant Bartholomew pretends to be Sly's wife and the Lord proposes that Sly and his 'wife' watch a play, which is the main action of *The Taming of the Shrew*.

In the first act, Lucentio arrives in Padua, with his attendant Tranio, in pursuit of an education, and quickly falls in love with Bianca, youngest daughter of Baptista Minola. Bianca is pursued by several suitors, but Baptista has decreed that she cannot marry until her older sister Katherina, the 'shrew', is married. Katherina, outspoken and feisty, presents an unappealing prospect for most suitors; however, this does not deter Petruchio, newly arrived in Padua to see his friend Hortensio and to look for a wife himself, so long as she is rich. Lucentio and Tranio devise a plan: Lucentio will disguise himself as 'Cambio', a schoolmaster, in order to gain access to Bianca, and Tranio will pretend to be Lucentio. Gremio and Hortensio, Bianca's suitors, are unimpressed with the arrival of 'Lucentio' (Tranio) as another rival, but the three agree to work together towards the common goal of helping Petruchio woo Katherina, in order to make way for a marriage to Bianca.

The second act opens with a fight between the two Minola sisters. Katherina has tied Bianca's hands, jealous of her father's favourite daughter. The suitors arrive at the house – Petruchio, Gremio, who unknowingly brings as a gift the rival Lucentio (disguised as 'Cambio'), Hortensio (disguised as 'Litio') and Tranio (disguised as Lucentio). After Baptista sends the 'tutors' in to his daughters, Katherina breaks a lute over Hortensio's head. In their first meeting, Petruchio and Katherina exchange insults but it is also apparent that they have much in common – intelligence, education and independent, contrary natures. Baptista agrees to their marriage, despite Katherina's objection that Petruchio is a lunatic. Tranio (as Lucentio) competes with Gremio to win Bianca's hand for his master, but now he will have to produce a rich father for Lucentio.

In the third act, the tutors compete for the attentions of Bianca, using lessons in Latin and music as a cover for conveying amorous messages to Bianca. By the end of the lessons, it appears that Lucentio is winning the competition. Hortensio is disheartened but considers wooing elsewhere. The wedding of Petruchio and Katherina goes ahead but does not run smoothly. The wedding party is kept waiting for the bridegroom. When the servant Biondello arrives, he gives a colourful report on what Petruchio is wearing. Finally, Petruchio arrives in his outlandish attire, ready for the ceremony. Meanwhile, Tranio plans to organise someone to impersonate Lucentio's father and Lucentio contemplates eloping with Bianca. Gremio gives an account of Petruchio's shrewish behaviour at the ceremony before the wedding party arrives. Petruchio denies Katherina the enjoyment of the wedding banquet, insisting they have to leave, and giving a speech about wives as the property of husbands.

In the fourth act, Petruchio arrives with Katherina at his country house and is excessively harsh and unreasonable with the servants, resulting in Katherina defending them. He denies Kate food and sleep, and reveals his taming strategy in a soliloquy to the audience. Hortensio abandons his pursuit of Bianca – since it is clear she only has eyes for 'Cambio' –

and decides to marry a wealthy widow instead, intending to train her using Petruchio's methods. After offering then denying Katherina fine dresses and a cap, Petruchio proposes they visit her family. On the way, he instructs her to agree with his contrary perspective of the world and eventually Kate enters into the spirit of the game. Meanwhile Tranio has tricked a merchant into pretending to be Lucentio's father Vincentio and takes him to Baptista, who agrees to the wedding between 'Lucentio' and Bianca. However, on the road Petruchio and Kate encounter the real Vincentio heading to Padua to see his son Lucentio, and Petruchio tells him of his son's marriage.

In the final act, Lucentio and Bianca marry secretly while Lucentio's father, the real Vincentio, confronts his imposter the Merchant. When the newlyweds return, they ask forgiveness of their two angry fathers. At the end of 5.1 there are signs that Katherina is warming to her new husband since Petruchio manages to obtain a kiss from her. In the final scene, Katherina and the Widow (Hortensio's new wife) clash over the Widow's assertion that Petruchio is troubled with a shrew. Petruchio proposes a bet among the men to see whose wife will obediently come when called. Although Bianca and the Widow refuse to come when called, Kate appears promptly, and furthermore gives an accomplished rhetorical performance on the subject of wifely obedience. Has 'the shrew' been tamed or is something more complex at play here?

Character summaries

The Induction (frame narrative)

Christopher Sly: a tinker (someone who mends pots and pans)

Hostess: manages an alehouse and argues with Sly

Lord: plays a trick on Sly

Bartholomew: the Lord's page (pretends to be Sly's wife)

The Taming of the Shrew (play-within-a-play)

Katherina: outspoken and defiant woman; eldest daughter of Baptista Minola

Petruchio: suitor to Katherina

Bianca: youngest daughter of Baptista; object of several suitors

Lucentio: suitor to Bianca; pretends to be 'Cambio'

Tranio: servant of Lucentio; pretends to be Lucentio

Hortensio: suitor to Bianca; pretends to be 'Litio'; love interest of the Widow

Gremio: suitor to Bianca; rich old man

Grumio: servant of Petruchio

Vincentio: father of Lucentio

Merchant: pretends to be Vincentio

Widow: in love with Hortensio

Biondello: additional servant of Lucentio

Curtis, Nathaniel, Philip, Joseph, Nicholas and Peter: additional servants of Petruchio

BACKGROUND & CONTEXT

The play's setting

The frame narrative is set in Warwickshire, England. Sly states that his father is of 'Burton-heath' and he refers to a 'fat ale-wife of Wincot' (Induction 2.16,18); both villages are close to Stratford-upon-Avon, where Shakespeare grew up. However, the play-within-a-play is set in Padua, Italy, the site of an old university – which is relevant to the theme of education that runs through the play.

Shakespeare's historical contexts

The position of women

Society has a long history of subjugating women; this was particularly evident in the early modern period, as reflected in the plays of Shakespeare and his contemporaries. Women at this time were perceived as socially and intellectually inferior to men, and it was assumed women belonged in the home so they were generally excluded from matters of state and warfare. Furthermore, women – who did not own property – were *treated* as property and passed from fathers to husbands. Thus, marriage was transactional. Women were expected to be silent, chaste and obedient. A main appeal of the play lies in Katherina's challenge to these expectations, and her voice and outspoken nature encapsulate the male fear of women.

In Shakespeare's period, there were no female actors allowed on stage. Women did not appear on stage until the Restoration period, from 1660. Thus, when *The Taming of the Shrew* was first performed, male actors played the female parts such as Katherina and Bianca. So, in one sense it gives the presentation of gender issues on stage the nature of a hypothetical debate among men, reflecting anxieties in the period about women becoming more assertive. Although not on the stage, women were in the audience, and the fact that the debate was taking place at all suggests that many women in the period did speak out and resist their husbands and the expectations of society.

The term 'shrew', or scold, was generally a term for an outspoken woman, and being thought a shrew could result in public punishment and humiliation. When in 1.1 Baptista attempts to persuade Bianca's suitors to consider Katherina instead, Gremio puns on 'court' by retorting: 'To cart her rather! She's too rough for me' (1.1.55). 'Cart' refers to the practice of publicly humiliating unruly women by conveying them through the streets on or behind a cart. Such practices underlined the sanctions against women speaking out. While it was most often a woman who was termed a shrew, in some contexts the word could also be applied to men, and Petruchio's contrary and difficult behaviour constructs him as a type of shrew.

Festival

The trick played on Sly, pretending that a lowborn person is highborn, is reminiscent of traditional English festival practices, such as appointing a Lord of Misrule, when someone of low status was temporarily elevated to a superior position for a day. Such practices functioned as a temporary release for a society that was constrained by hierarchy and rigid rules. Temporary festive rituals provided enjoyment and created comedy in their transgressive breaking of the rules. However, ultimately such games reaffirmed the normal rules of society.

Commedia dell'arte

The Italian theatrical tradition of *commedia dell'arte*, which involves improvisation, stock characters and masks, strongly influenced European theatre from the mid-sixteenth century to the mid-eighteenth century. This tradition informs several of the characters and their relationships in the play. For example, the character Gremio, a rich old man described as a 'pantaloon' (3.1.35), is indebted to a stock character in *commedia dell'arte*, functioning as an obstacle for young lovers. Another common figure of the *commedia dell'arte* tradition is a wise and resourceful servant, such as Tranio.

Humours

The human body was thought to be composed of four substances, known as humours: blood, choler, melancholy and phlegm. Different characteristics were associated with each of these substances, and the proportions of the four humours in a person dictated their personality. Imbalances in the humours were believed to cause adverse health effects and particular behaviours. In the second part of the Induction, the Messenger pretends to Sly that his supposed illness, imagining he is lowborn, is the result of melancholy: 'Seeing too much sadness hath congealed your blood' (Induction 2.127) and that his doctors have thus prescribed a play as a type of medicine. In 4.1 Petruchio rejects the meat dish by relying on the theory of the four humours. He claims that burnt meat 'engenders choler, planteth anger' and that 'ourselves are choleric' (4.1.143, 145), that is, prone to anger.

Mythology

The English Renaissance period (from the late 1500s to 1660) was one of intense literary productivity that included a revival of interest in classical Greek and Roman literature. English Renaissance literature commonly refers to tales of gods and goddesses from classical mythology. Such references may aim to flatter a person or elevate a situation, or they may be used for parody and comic effect. References to Greek and Roman gods are often a mark of education, evidencing the speaker's knowledge. In the Induction, the Lord refers to Apollo, the god of music and the sun (Induction 2.31), displaying his education and thus higher status; even the Lord's servants assail Sly with mythological references that Sly is unlikely to understand. Lucentio compares his love for Bianca to that of Jove for Europa (1.1.160). Other references include 'Sibyl' (1.2.67), an aged prophetess in classical mythology, to whom Petruchio refers in order to claim that even an old woman would not deter him from his wooing. Tranio compares Bianca to 'Leda's daughter' (1.2.237), Helen of Troy, which is ironic since Helen's beauty and desirability was the cause of the Trojan war. Bianca's beauty and her suitors' attempts to become her husband don't cause a war, but they do create drama and humour. Petruchio compares Katherina to 'Dian' (2.1.248), the virgin goddess of the hunt, thus praising her while also referencing her war-like nature.

The publication history of *The Taming of the Shrew*

There are no surviving draft manuscripts, notes or diaries left by Shakespeare, so scholars have to piece together other evidence to determine approximately when a play was written. *The Taming of the Shrew* is believed to have been written around 1590–91 and in existence by 1592, making it one of Shakespeare's earliest plays.

The dating of Shakespeare's play is complicated by the existence of a similar play – *The Taming of a Shrew* – published anonymously in quarto editions (a cheaper, smaller format) in 1594, 1596 and 1607. This may have been a plagiarised version of Shakespeare's play. Shakespeare's *Shrew* was not published until the First Folio in 1623. Folio was a larger, more expensive format and the 1623 First Folio was the first collected edition of Shakespeare's plays.

GENRE, STRUCTURE & LANGUAGE

Genre

In the 1623 First Folio, the editors divided the plays into three genres: comedies, tragedies and histories. *The Taming of the Shrew* is a comedy. A Shakespearean comedy is classified as such not because it is funny – even though the comedies include many humorous scenes – but because the plot resolves in marriage. In a comedy, various pairs of lovers undergo trials and obstacles to ultimately end up together. The obstacle for young lovers to overcome generally lies with the older generation, fathers or other patriarchal figures. Grumio refers to this familiar pattern of comedy when he says: 'Here's no knavery! See, to beguile the old folks, how the young folks lay their heads together' (1.2.132–3). Ironically, he says this just as Gremio, the old suitor of Bianca, enters with Lucentio in disguise as Cambio; the foolish Gremio is unaware that he is introducing a new suitor for Bianca.

Although *Shrew* is a comedy, the main pair of 'lovers' is not a typical romantic couple; for most of the play they are locked in a battle of wits and power play. The conventional language of love that Bianca's suitors use stands in stark contrast to the insults of the battling Katherina and Petruchio. So Shakespeare takes the genre of comedy and challenges it, pushing it to its limits.

In terms of Shakespeare's sources, the main plot originates in folklore. The frame narrative of Sly becoming a lord for a day also derives from folklore and festive practices. There were various ballads on the theme of husbands dealing with unruly wives, including *A Merry Jest of a Shrewd and Cursed Wife* (1550), and Erasmus' 'A Merry Dialogue, Declaring the Properties of Shrewd Shrews and Honest Wives', translated in 1557. Lucentio's wooing of Bianca can be traced to George Gascoigne's comedy *Supposes* (1566), a translation of the Italian poet Ariosto's *I suppositi* (1509).

Structure

The key structural feature is the play-within-a-play. The main story of the taming of a shrew is itself a play that Christopher Sly and others are watching, part of a trick played on him to make him think he is a lord. We become so absorbed in the inset play that we tend to forget that it is distinct from the frame narrative. Shakespeare himself appears to have become similarly absorbed in the shrew narrative, to the extent that he seems to have abandoned the frame narrative, and we do not see Sly again after 1.1.

The play-within-a-play is a common dramatic device that Shakespeare uses in several of his works, such as *Hamlet* and *A Midsummer Night's Dream*. The effect of this device is often described as 'metadramatic' or 'metatheatrical' because it draws attention to the process of drama and the nature of theatre itself. It reminds the audience that they are watching a play, thus temporarily breaking the illusion of the world that the play creates.

The frame narrative envelops the main plot. This adds an additional layer of complexity to our reading of the play. Is the shrew narrative merely a drunken dream of Sly's, the 'taming' of an assertive woman intended to be a ridiculous fantasy like that of the lowborn Sly imagining he is a lord? Perhaps Petruchio's 'taming' of a shrew is merely Sly's imagined revenge on the Hostess for throwing him out of the tavern.

Language

Shakespeare was a gifted wordsmith, inventing many new words and playing on the multiple meanings of a word. Shifts in a conversation often hinge on a word used in one sense by one character, then in a different sense by another. His language can be difficult when encountered for the first time; some words that were common when he was writing are now unfamiliar. Other words may be familiar but their meaning has changed over time. For example, when Petruchio calls his servant Grumio 'villain'

(1.2.8), this is a reference to a lower-class person or a labourer, not an evil person. The vocabulary lists, both in this guide and in editions of the text, will help you to interpret unfamiliar words.

You will notice Shakespeare's constant use of **metaphors** to describe people, emotions and events. This technique, common in Renaissance literature, adds depth and complexity to the language of the play through the mental images that the words evoke. For example, when Tranio says to Petruchio, ''Tis thought your deer does hold you at a bay' (5.2.56), the metaphor of Katherina as a deer conveys that wooing is a type of hunting. Also watch for **similes**, which use 'as' or 'like' to set up a comparison. For example, when Lucentio first arrives in Padua he says, 'for I have Pisa left / And am to Padua come as he that leaves / A shallow plash to plunge him in the deep / And with satiety seeks to quench his thirst' (1.1.21–4). This conveys that he has moved from his smaller home town with a thirst for knowledge and for the greater opportunities of Padua. Petruchio uses a simile when he argues that he is not deterred by a shrewish wife: 'She moves me not, or not removes at least / Affection's edge in me, were she as rough / As are the swelling Adriatic seas' (1.2.69–71).

Note the use of **sibilance**, a particular type of **alliteration** using the 's' sound, such as in Tranio's: 'your resolve / To suck the sweets of sweet philosophy' (1.1.27–8). Many characters also use **punning**, playing with multiple meanings of a word; for example, when Curtis says, 'I call them forth to credit her' and Grumio replies, 'Why, she comes to borrow nothing of them' (4.1.78–9), Grumio plays on the different meanings of credit. When Lucentio says 'And let me be a slave t'achieve that maid / Whose sudden sight hath thralled my wounded eye' (1.1.210–11), he plays on two types of enslavement – servitude and the idea of being enslaved through love.

In *The Taming of the Shrew*, a key aspect of language is the way it is used in **insults**. Insults can be part of lighthearted banter (as in an exchange between friends) and may be ironic, carrying the opposite of their apparent meaning, such as Grumio calling the old Gremio 'a proper stripling' (1.2.137), a handsome youth. Insults can also be deadly serious and suggest or lead to physical violence. Note the violence implied when Grumio, Petruchio's servant, describes how his master is capable of withstanding Katherina's insults; words like 'throw a figure' and 'disfigure her' (1.2.108) suggest that insults are like physical violence.

Katherina uses insults as part of her resistance to the patriarchal assumptions that constrain women. She and Petruchio trade insults as part of their feisty courtship. In their encounter at 2.1, their rapid firing of words constitutes **stichomythia** (when alternating lines of dialogue are spoken by different characters), increasing the dramatic interest of the scene. Petruchio counters Katherina's verbal assaults and demonstrates that he is a witty and intelligent potential partner for her. In matching each other's insults, often using the last comment as a springboard for the next, they paradoxically demonstrate their suitability for each other.

As you are reading the play, note the rhythm of the language. Most of the upper-class characters speak in verse, while the lower-class characters speak in prose. The verse lines are in iambic pentameter: there are five 'beats' or stressed syllables in each line, with one unstressed syllable before each stressed syllable. This pattern gives a sense of overall order. Sometimes there are 'missing' beats to the pentameter line, which creates particular effects. For example, when Baptista says 'Go in, Bianca' (1.1.91), this fills only two beats of the line – so the extra three beats' silence allows for Bianca to leave the stage before Baptista speaks to the others who remain.

Changes between prose and verse can be used to convey information about the characters. Sly speaks in prose, not verse – showing his lower-class status – in contrast to the verse spoken by the Lord. However, as Sly comes to believe in the trick, entering into the delusion, he too begins to speak in verse (from Induction 2.64). That Sly is able to speak in verse at all suggests the idea that class is constructed, a type of performance, like gender.

In some conversations between characters, you will note that there are two half-lines that seem connected. The two speeches, or shared line, *together* create a single line of iambic pentameter, forming five beats between them. This unity of rhythm parallels particular connections between characters at certain points. For example, Kate's 'You were a movable' is completed by Petruchio's 'Why, what's a movable?' (2.1.193), signalling their connection.

Shakespeare also has his characters use the rhetorical device of **anaphora**: repetition of a word or phrase at the beginning of a line, used for emphasis. For example, Petruchio says 'Have I not in my time heard lions roar? / Have I not heard the sea, puffed up with winds' (1.2.194–5).

You may also notice that some lines seem to stand out from the text as memorable quotations that could be used outside of the play. In Shakespeare's time, proverbs and aphorisms were popular; these are short sayings, usually with a didactic function (trying to teach a moral lesson). Shakespeare's audience often took notes of useful lines they could add to their commonplace books (compilations of useful sayings). Some examples are: 'And frame your mind to mirth and merriment, / Which bars a thousand harms and lengthens life' (Induction 2.130–1); and 'let the world slip. We shall ne'er be younger' (Induction 2.139).

SCENE-BY-SCENE ANALYSIS

The Induction (frame narrative)

Summary: *Sly, a tinker, argues with an alehouse Hostess. After waking from a drunken stupor, Sly becomes the victim of a practical joke in which a Lord pretends that Sly is a rich lord with a wife and offers him the entertainment of a play.*

The play begins with an argument between Christopher Sly, a drunken tinker, and the hostess of an alehouse. Sly's claim to noble lineage and his use of Latin to try to establish some dignity is immediately undermined by the fact that he confuses the biblical figure of St Jerome with a character from a play. After refusing to pay for some broken glasses, Sly passes out drunk outside the alehouse. A Lord enters after hunting, a typical aristocratic pursuit. He devises a trick whereby he will pretend that low-born Sly is actually a nobleman, that he has a wife (Bartholomew, the Lord's page) and that Sly has had a period of insanity for the past seven years, during which he imagined that he was a 'poor and loathsome beggar' (Induction 1.119). The Lord is amused at the thought of this mock homage to a man of low status. He proposes a play about the taming of a shrew be performed for Lord Sly.

Giving Sly the temporary life of a lord has a comic effect but also implicitly makes us question, as an audience, the basis for such stark differences in the status of people. The comic effect of Sly believing that he could in fact be a lord suggests that the way we treat people affects their behaviour and the identity they assume: 'He is no less than what we say he is' (Induction 1.67). That is, identity can be shaped by labelling.

The Lord's advice to Bartholomew on how to be a dutiful wife is, ironically, one man's advice to another man (which reflects that fact that all female characters in the play were played by male actors). This introduces a theme of the main inset play: the social roles of women.

In the second part of the Induction, at the Lord's country house, Sly is waited on before the entertainment. Class difference is conveyed in the type of drink Sly orders; he asks for small ale but he is offered sack, a more refined drink. Sly's reference to 'bear-herd' (Induction 2.17) recalls the bear-baiting that took place in the vicinity of the Globe theatre. This contrasts with the mythological and historical references that the Lord makes. There is a stark contrast between the fiction that they are trying to lure Sly into and his reality.

Sly is bewildered as to what is fact or fantasy: 'Am I a lord, and have I such a lady? / Or do I dream? Or have I dreamed till now?' (Induction 2.64–5). He begins to speak in verse, like an upper-class person (Induction 2.64–71), although he undermines this effect by calling for his pot of small ale, signalling that he remains himself. The serving men attempt to unsettle Sly's memory, referring to him being thrown out of the tavern as a false memory, and denying the existence of Sly's acquaintances.

In the second part of the Induction, the characters enter 'aloft'. The Globe theatre had three levels that had practical and symbolic implications. There was the main playing stage, with an inset area at the back; a trapdoor, which characters could appear from or descend into; and a raised area above the main stage. This is where Sly and the others enter to become an onstage audience for the inset play.

Key point

The presence of the frame narrative raises questions about the theme of the play. Is the idea of the taming of a shrew supposed to represent a fantasy of Sly's, something that he might dream of doing, but which is intended to be as ridiculous an idea as that of Sly being a lord? If so, how does that change our thoughts about themes presented in the main play?

Key vocabulary

paucas pallabris (1.4): few words

denier (1.7): French coin of low value

thirdborough (1.9): officer

brach (1.14): bitch

belike (1.71): perhaps

over-merry spleen (1.133): excessive impulse to laughter

sack (2.2): sherry or dry white wine (a more refined drink than ale)

cardmaker (2.17): worker in the wool trade

Apollo (2.31): god of music

Semiramis (2.35): Assyrian queen

bestrow (2.36): scatter

welkin (2.41): sky, heavens

Adonis (2.46): mortal lover of Aphrodite/Venus

Cytherea (2.47): Aphrodite/Venus, goddess of love

Io (2.50): mortal loved by Zeus and transformed into a cow

Daphne (2.53): nymph loved by Apollo and transformed into a laurel tree

Q If it is possible to create a 'lord' out of Sly, however fleeting, what does this suggest about class status in society?

Act 1

1.1 Summary: *Lucentio and his attendant Tranio arrive in Padua. They encounter the Minola family with the outspoken Katherina and the obedient daughter Bianca. Lucentio quickly falls in love with Bianca and he and Tranio plan to swap roles so Lucentio can gain access to Bianca.*

Lucentio and Tranio have left Pisa for Padua, a centre of learning, to pursue an education. Lucentio proposes to study philosophy, in particular 'happiness / By virtue specially to be achieved' (1.1.19–20), an idea from the classical philosopher Aristotle. Tranio proves just as knowledgeable as Lucentio, for he recognises Aristotle's idea but argues that they should not forget about pleasure, bringing in a reference to Ovid, a Roman poet famous for writing on the theme of love and for the work *Metamorphoses*, on the Greek myths. Lucentio and Tranio then stand aside as the Minola family enter, thus creating another layer of spectators.

Baptista outlines his rule: 'That is, not to bestow my youngest daughter / Before I have a husband for the elder' (1.1.50–1). Baptista is a type of blocking figure, common in Shakespeare's comedies, where young lovers have to find a way around parental opposition to their union. Baptista invites Gremio and Hortensio to consider courting Katherina; however, they are unconvinced.

Katherina challenges her father's attempts to marry her off: 'is it your will / To make a stale of me amongst these mates?' (1.1.57–8). The word 'stale' (sometimes meaning prostitute) suggests that trading a woman in marriage for a dowry parallels prostitution. Kate also threatens physical violence (1.1.64–5). Hortensio labels outspoken women as demonic – 'all such devils' (1.1.66) – while Tranio observes that Kate is either 'stark mad, or wonderful froward' (1.1.69).

Hortensio and Gremio complain about Bianca being sent inside; however, Baptista's plan to engage tutors for her creates an opportunity. Lucentio uses conventional language to express his love of Bianca while Tranio tries to point out the obstacle of Kate. They hatch a plan to swap roles – Tranio will pretend to be Lucentio so Lucentio can pretend to be a tutor for Bianca.

At the scene's end, the Lord notes that Sly is nodding off. Sly asks his 'wife' Bartholomew if the play is nearly finished, but she informs him that it has only just begun. After this point, Shakespeare doesn't return to the frame narrative so we do not find out what Sly thinks of the play, or even whether he stays awake.

1.2 Summary: *Petruchio arrives in Padua to seek a wife and see his friend Hortensio. Petruchio resolves to woo Katherina, despite his friend's warning, since she is rich and he is up for a challenge. Gremio unwittingly engages 'Cambio' (Lucentio in disguise) as tutor to Bianca, and the three suitors to Bianca – Gremio, Hortensio and Tranio (in disguise as Lucentio) – are pleased that Petruchio will clear the way for their suits.*

Petruchio arrives from Verona with his servant Grumio to visit friends in Padua, particularly Hortensio. He has also come to seek a wife; his father has died, leaving him an inheritance, and he is interested in making an advantageous marriage. Hortensio immediately suggests Katherina, initially in jest, and Petruchio is keen. His only motivation seems to be money at this stage, so he is not deterred by Hortensio's negative descriptions of Katherina. Grumio knows his master Petruchio well and reflects that Katherina's scolding would have little effect on him. Hortensio confesses that he is in love with Bianca and outlines the situation to Petruchio: 'Therefore this order hath Baptista tane, / That none shall have access unto Bianca / Till Katherine the curst have got a husband' (1.2.120–2). Hortensio outlines his plan to disguise himself as a music tutor so he can gain access to Bianca.

At that moment, Gremio, Hortensio's rival, arrives with Lucentio, disguised as a schoolmaster, Cambio. Gremio is keen to engage a scholar for Bianca in order to please Baptista, but he is unaware that he is admitting a rival suitor into Bianca's company. Ironically, Grumio's comment on the young beguiling the old (1.2.132–3) comes just prior to the entry of the foolish old Gremio with Lucentio. Gremio instructs Lucentio to read books on the topic of love to Bianca, and Lucentio pretends that he will advocate for Gremio's suit.

Gremio advises Hortensio that he has found a tutor for Bianca and Hortensio tells Gremio that he has found a suitor for Katherina in Petruchio. Tranio arrives, disguised as Lucentio. Gremio and Hortensio are concerned lest Tranio prove another rival for Bianca; while Petruchio, comically, is concerned that he may be a rival for Katherina. The act ends with the three rivals for Bianca united in gratitude for Petruchio paving the way for them through his wooing of Katherina. Tranio proposes that they 'contrive this afternoon / And quaff carouses to our mistress' health, / And do as adversaries do in law, / Strive mightily, but eat and drink as friends' (1.2.269–72).

Key point

The first act sets up dramatic expectation for the encounter between Petruchio and Katherina in Act 2. Petruchio contributes to this through a poetic and evocative narrative of how he has bravely encountered challenging situations before:

> Think you a little din can daunt mine ears?
> Have I not in my time heard lions roar?
> Have I not heard the sea, puffed up with winds,
> Rage like an angry boar chafèd with sweat?
> Have I not heard great ordnance in the field,
> And heaven's artillery thunder in the skies?
> Have I not in a pitchèd battle heard
> Loud 'larums, neighing steeds and trumpets' clang?
> And do you tell me of a woman's tongue,
> That gives not half so great a blow to hear
> As will a chestnut in a farmer's fire?
> Tush, tush, fear boys with bugs! (1.2.193–204)

The speech equates encountering a scolding woman with experiencing wild beasts, storms and war, at which Petruchio scoffs. The stage is thus set for him to meet his future wife.

Key vocabulary

Balk logic (1.1.34): bandy words

Gramercies (1.1.41): many thanks

pantaloon (1.1.46): ridiculous old man; stock figure from *commedia dell'arte*

Iwis (1.1.62): certainly

froward (1.1.69): disobedient; headstrong

peat (1.1.78): spoilt child

Minerva (1.1.84): goddess of wisdom

brooked parle (1.1.112): enabled negotiations

lief (1.1.126): willingly

Redime ... minimo (1.1.153): ransom yourself, now that you've been captured, for as low a price as you can

daughter of Agenor (1.1.159): Europa, abducted by Jove in the form of a bull

Jove (1.1.160): Jupiter; leader of the Roman gods; the Greek equivalent is Zeus

Basta (1.1.189): enough (Italian)

Saint Anne (1.1.240): mother of the Virgin Mary

rebused (1.2.7): Grumio's mistaken term for abused

Con ... trovato (1.2.23): with all my heart well met (Italian)

Alla ... Petruchio (1.2.24–5): welcome to our house, much-honoured Signor Petruchio (Italian)

Florentius's love (1.2.66): reference to a knight who married an ugly old woman to save his life

Sibyl (1.2.67): aged prophetess in classical mythology

Xanthippe (1.2.68): bad-tempered wife of the Greek philosopher Socrates

aglet-baby (1.2.75): small carved figure

proper stripling (1.2.137): handsome youth

bugs (1.2.204): fantasy figures, hobgoblins

Leda's daughter (1.2.237): Helen of Troy, cause of the Trojan War when Paris abducted her from her husband

Paris (1.2.240): Trojan prince who stole Helen

prove a jade (1.2.242): soon tire (like an old horse)

Alcides' twelve (1.2.251): the twelve difficult labours of Hercules

quaff carouses (1.2.270): drink toasts

Q What kind of a character is Petruchio, based on the evidence of the first act?

Q Analyse the ways in which Katherina is labelled in this first act. What do you think the effect of labelling is on people?

Act 2

2.1 Summary: *Katherina torments Bianca, giving vent to her jealousy and frustration. After Baptista sends the 'tutors' to his daughters, Katherina breaks a lute over Hortensio's head. Petruchio and Katherina meet and trade insults but Baptista agrees to their marriage. Tranio (as Lucentio) outbids Gremio for Bianca's hand, but now must produce Lucentio's father.*

The scene opens in the middle of a physical fight between Katherina and Bianca. Katherina has bound Bianca's hands; the binding and Bianca's reference to 'bondmaid' and 'slave' (2.1.2) are symbolic of the constraints that she will experience in being married, and also her controlled state as an obedient daughter. Bianca says she will do whatever Katherina commands since 'So well I know my duty to my elders' (2.1.7). Katherina demands to know which of Bianca's suitors she loves best and this indicates the source of Katherina's rage: her jealousy of her sister's popularity. Bianca pleads with her sister to untie her but Katherina hits her. Baptista enters and releases Bianca, describing Katherina as a 'devilish spirit!' (2.1.26). After the exit of the daughters, the suitors enter (with three of them in disguise).

Petruchio describes Katherina in a way that is clearly contrary to her reputation, including phrases such as 'affability' and 'mild behaviour' (2.1.48, 49). Petruchio presents 'Litio' (Hortensio) from Mantua as a tutor for Katherina in music and mathematics. Gremio presents 'Cambio' (Lucentio) as a tutor for Bianca, claiming he is a scholar from Rheims skilled in Greek, Latin and other languages. 'Lucentio' (Tranio) presents himself as a visitor from Pisa and a suitor to Bianca, presenting a gift of a lute as well as Greek and Latin books. Baptista sends the tutors in to his daughters while he talks with Petruchio. Their discussion of money highlights the way that marriage was a type of financial transaction, yet both men seem to know that Katherina's consent is needed. Petruchio says 'if I get your daughter's love' (2.1.115) and Baptista says 'Ay, when the special thing is well obtained, / That is, her love, for that is all in all'

(2.1.124–5). Petruchio appears confident of gaining Katherina's love and is undaunted by her reputation: 'For I am rough and woo not like a babe' (2.1.133). Baptista is doubtful and warns 'But be thou armed for some unhappy words' (2.1.135).

Hortensio enters with the lute broken on his head. Since playing the lute was an appropriate feminine accomplishment for middle- to upper-class women, Katherina smashing the lute on Hortensio's head encapsulates what she thinks of such expectations. Clearly the music lesson has not gone well, but Petruchio is not discouraged. In a soliloquy he outlines his strategy; in response to her hostility, he plans to act as if she has behaved in the opposite manner.

When Katherina enters, Petruchio shortens her name to the more familiar Kate and repeats it in multiple ways, including with implied puns, such as when he mentions 'dainties' (2.1.185), meaning delicacies, sometimes called 'cates'. He flatters her, calling her 'the prettiest Kate in Christendom' (2.1.183). They then engage in a battle of wits. When Petruchio says, 'Myself am moved to woo thee for my wife' (2.1.190), Kate responds with 'Let him that moved you hither / Remove you hence' (2.1.191–2). She also accuses him of being 'a movable' (2.1.193), a changeable person, yet this is the first clue that she would rather have him constant. Note that this occurs in the couple's first shared line together, signalling a connection. When she insults him, calling him a 'joint stool' (2.1.194), he shifts it to a flirtatious invitation to come and sit on him, creating another shared line. The conversation continues in this vein, and through their complex wordplay, which displays both their intelligence and their education, they find that they are in fact compatible.

The battle of words becomes physical. Kate's 'If I be waspish, best beware my sting' (2.1.206) leads to a series of retorts ending with Petruchio's bawdy inuendo of 'my tongue in your tail?' (2.1.212). Katherina strikes him but he holds her in response. Petruchio maintains his strategy; despite her insults, he praises her: 'For thou art pleasant, gamesome, passing courteous' (2.1.235). Thus, he demonstrates *his* ability to be contrary. Katherina expresses her astonishment at Petruchio's talent with words: 'Where did you study all this goodly speech?' (2.1.252). She is surprised to meet someone with the same verbal skills in insults and puns as herself.

Petruchio tells Katherina that her father has consented to their marriage, and she criticises her father for agreeing to her being 'wed to one half lunatic' (2.1.276). Petruchio continues in his contrary vein, asserting that they have agreed the wedding day. He makes the insightful observation that 'If she be curst, it is for policy' (2.1.281); that is, she deliberately chooses to be contrary. While Petruchio's assertion that they get on well together is, on the surface, ironic, at a deeper level it reflects that a connection has been created between them.

The scene is particularly humorous when Petruchio claims that it is 'incredible to believe / How much she loves me' (2.1.295–6) and describes how Kate was making amorous advances to him. He claims that they have agreed that she will only be 'curst in company' (2.1.294); that is, when others are around, she will pretend to be hostile. Baptista is almost speechless, and Petruchio announces that he will go to Venice to buy things for the wedding.

After Petruchio and Katherina exit separately, Baptista reflects on the risks of the match. Bianca's suitors are now free to put forward their competing claims. Gremio claims a right since he was first; however, Tranio (as Lucentio) insists that he loves Bianca more. The juxtaposition of 'freeze' and 'fry' (2.1.327) in a line shared by the suitors encapsulates the opposition of the old and young suitors. Baptista continues to put money first and says he will award Bianca to whomever can offer the greatest financial security. The suitors then compete by outlining their wealth. Gremio, as a rich old man, is best placed to offer a substantial package and his speech evokes the early modern world of trade: 'Tyrian tapestry' (2.1.338), 'Turkey cushions' (2.1.342) and 'Valance of Venice' (2.1.343). These give a sense of the goods that were traded and available to wealthy households. Bianca, however, is not consulted.

Tranio (as Lucentio), in order to compete with Gremio, has to make a grander claim. He points out that as his father's heir and only son, he stands to inherit a sizeable fortune. Tranio wins the bidding war and Baptista promises Bianca to him. Once Tranio is alone he reflects that, although he has won the competition, he now has to make good his claims and produce a father for 'Lucentio', which will require a further disguise. Tranio uses the analogy of a card game; his bluff (pretending he has a higher-value hand of cards than he actually has) is called and he now has to meet the expectations he has created.

Key point

Katherina's last line of Act 2 is 'I'll see thee hanged on Sunday first!' (2.1.288), in response to Petruchio's claim that the following Sunday will be the wedding day. After Baptista agrees to the match, and Petruchio asks Katherina for a kiss, there are no lines or stage directions to give an indication of what Katherina thinks. How does she feel about her father agreeing to the match? How does she respond to the kiss? These are questions that directors and actors have to decide on.

Key vocabulary

gauds (2.1.3): adornments

raiment (2.1.5): clothes

dissemble (2.1.9): cheat, lie

lead apes in hell (2.1.34): since older unmarried women had no children to lead into heaven

Backare (2.1.72): stand back (mock Latin)

fain (2.1.73): gladly, willingly

pillory (2.1.152): punishment device that clamped an offender's head and hands

joint stool (2.1.194): wooden stool, insult

tane (2.1.202): taken, caught in flight (term from falconry)

turtle (2.1.204): turtle-dove, symbol of love

crest (2.1.219): heraldic device or tuft of feathers on bird's head

coxcomb (2.1.219): fool's cap (which resembles the crest of a rooster)

crab (2.1.224): sour crabapple

Dian (2.1.248): Diana, goddess of hunting and chastity

Grissel (2.1.284): famously obedient wife

Lucrece (2.1.285): legendary Roman woman famed for her chastity who killed herself after being raped by King Tarquin

meacock (2.1.302): mild, timid

Skipper (2.1.328): playboy, irresponsible youth

lave (2.1.337): wash

argosy (2.1.363): large merchant ship

Q Analyse the verbal battle of wits between Katherina and Petruchio. Which literary techniques, such as punning, alliteration and rhyme, does the sparring pair use and what do these reveal about their interactions?

Q Consider the way Baptista deals with the suitors for his daughters. What does this suggest about the position of women in early modern society?

Act 3

3.1 Summary: *Lucentio (as Cambio) defeats Hortensio (as Litio) in competing for the attentions of Bianca.*

Hortensio uses hyperbole to flatter Bianca, calling her the 'patroness of heavenly harmony' (3.1.5), which refers to the Renaissance idea of the music of the spheres. He wants Bianca to have an hour of music before listening to Lucentio's lecture. However, Lucentio declares that the lecture in philosophy should come first. Bianca says that it should be her choice what she studies, showing a trace of her sister's assertiveness. Bianca settles the dispute by saying that she will listen to the philosophy lecture while Hortensio tunes his lute. Lucentio reads Latin, which was the traditional language of learning, using this as a cover, pretending to translate sections of Latin while in fact conveying his feelings to Bianca. She wittily answers him, keeping him at a distance – 'presume not' – yet also keeping his hopes alive – 'despair not' (3.1.41, 42).

Meanwhile, Hortensio claims his instrument is now in tune and ready to go, which Lucentio disputes, suspecting Hortensio's motives, particularly as Hortensio's instructions (3.1.61–2) have a potentially bawdy innuendo. Hortensio uses the musical scale as a cover to convey his intentions to Bianca, but she is not receptive. A servant summons Bianca to help prepare for Katherina's wedding and, after Lucentio leaves, Hortensio has a brief soliloquy ending with a rhyming couplet that suggests that if Bianca's interests wander beyond him then he will look elsewhere. His words – 'stale' and 'ranging' – (3.1.87, 88) include the language of falconry; hunting was often used as a metaphor for wooing in the period.

3.2 Summary: *The wedding party awaits the late bridegroom; Katherina exits in tears. Biondello reports on Petruchio's outlandish attire before Petruchio finally arrives. Tranio plans to organise someone to impersonate Lucentio's father while Lucentio contemplates eloping with Bianca. Gremio provides a comic account of the wedding ceremony before the others arrive. Petruchio denies Katherina the wedding banquet and insists they leave.*

The Minola family and attendants assemble outside Baptista's house ready for the wedding, but Petruchio does not arrive. Katherina wittily reverses a common proverb: 'Who wooed in haste and means to wed at leisure' (3.2.11). Although she appears hostile to Petruchio, the fact that she is waiting for him in her wedding dress and that she exits weeping when he does not come suggests that, despite her show of opposition to the marriage, she does in fact want to marry him. Biondello arrives and gives a comic description of Petruchio's attire, which is the opposite of what would be expected of a groom – 'a monster, a very monster in apparel' (3.2.61–2). When Petruchio finally arrives, Baptista criticises him for appearing 'unprovided' (3.2.89), meaning unprepared for the wedding, which to Baptista's mind brings 'shame to [Petruchio's] estate' (3.2.90) and mocks the 'solemn festival' (3.2.91) of the wedding. Petruchio's contrary attitude to wooing and custom demonstrates that he does not care for society's opinion or traditions. He thus demonstrates a solidarity with Kate, who also resists societal expectations.

Petruchio rejects Tranio's suggestion to get changed; he scoffs at outward appearances, claiming, 'To me she's married, not unto my clothes' (3.2.107) – a suggestion that he values authenticity over superficiality. Tranio deduces that Petruchio has a purpose: 'He hath some meaning in his mad attire' (3.2.114). Petruchio exits, with Baptista following him. Meanwhile Tranio tells Lucentio that he will organise someone to impersonate Vincentio of Pisa, Lucentio's father, and Lucentio contemplates eloping with Bianca.

Gremio enters and gives an account of the wedding ceremony. Note that he describes Petruchio as a devil and Tranio likewise calls Katherina a devil (3.2.145, 46), emphasising the connection between the newlyweds. Gremio's opinion has now shifted and he sees Petruchio as worse than Katherina; he describes Petruchio's outrageous behaviour at the wedding ceremony – swearing and cuffing the priest, quaffing wine and throwing the dregs at the priest. As Gremio aptly says, 'Such a mad marriage never was before!' (3.2.172). When the wedding party enters, Petruchio continues with his contrary behaviour by, instead of following the usual custom of a wedding feast, insisting that they must leave straight away, meaning that poor Kate is denied the enjoyment of the feast. She tries pleading with him – 'Now, if you love me, stay' – to which he replies, 'Grumio, my horse!' (3.2.194), hardly the expected response of a bridegroom. Yet the shared line highlights their connection. Grumio emphasises the topsy-turvy world that the couple creates: 'the oats have eaten the horses' (3.2.195). Note also the gap in Kate's speech after 'Nay then' (3.2.196), which puns on the horses (neigh); there is a silence of four feet in which she is considering whether to challenge Petruchio or not, before she does decide to resist, with, 'I see a woman may be made a fool / If she had not a spirit to resist' (3.2.209–10).

Petruchio gives a speech that encapsulates the patriarchal attitude towards women in the early modern period, one that sees women as property (3.2.218–21). He pretends that Katherina needs rescuing and exits with her. After they exit, Baptista enters into the spirit of irony, calling them 'a couple of quiet ones!' (3.2.229). Bianca also discerns the likeness between Katherina and Petruchio: 'That being mad herself, she's madly mated' (3.2.233). Similarly, Gremio comments, 'Petruchio is Kated' (3.2.234), that is, Petruchio has become a shrew. In the absence of Petruchio and Katherina at the wedding feast, Baptista suggests that Tranio (as Lucentio) take the bridegroom's place and Bianca take her sister's place (3.2.238–9), thus foreshadowing their eventual wedding (and in another topsy-turvy moment, their wedding feast comes before their wedding).

Key point

Note how Biondello's description of what Petruchio is wearing has a greater comic effect than if Petruchio had simply appeared. Shakespeare's language in fact dresses Petruchio and enhances the impact of the costume. Likewise, Shakespeare chooses not to stage the wedding ceremony itself, so the episode is one of telling, from Gremio's account, rather than showing, thus building up expectation for when the wedding party arrives.

Key vocabulary

Conster (3.1.30): translate

Spit in the hole (3.1.38): try again (spit on your hands and take a better hold)

Pedascule (3.1.47): little pedant

Aeacides/Ajax (3.1.49, 50): Greek warrior at the siege of Troy

gamut (3.1.64): formal musical scale

stale (3.1.87): falconry term for a bird decoy; lure

chapeless (3.2.44): without a scabbard or sheath

glanders (3.2.46): disease causing swelling of the jaw and discharge from the nostrils

lampass/fashions (3.2.47, 48): diseases affecting an animal's mouth

staggers (3.2.49): disease causing giddiness

begnawn with the bots (3.2.50): eaten by intestinal worms

prodigy (3.2.86): omen

gogs-wouns (3.2.150): God's wounds (an oath)

cozen (3.2.158): cheat

buckler (3.2.228): shield

Q How does the wooing of Bianca at the beginning of Act 3 compare with the earlier wooing scene of Katherina by Petruchio in Act 2?

Q Why does Petruchio delay his arrival at the wedding and wear ridiculous clothes?

Act 4

4.1 Summary: *Grumio and the servants at Petruchio's country house prepare for his arrival. Petruchio chastises his servants, leading Katherina to defend them. Petruchio denies Kate food and sleep, and outlines his taming strategy to the audience.*

The servants, as lower-class characters, speak in prose, not verse. There is comic interplay when Grumio asks Curtis to 'Lend thine ear' (4.1.43) and then boxes Curtis' ear; their slapstick behaviour, with its emphasis on physicality, echoes that of their master and mistress. Grumio tells the tale of their journey: Katherina's horse stumbled; Kate fell into the mud and, instead of assisting her, Petruchio beat Grumio, resulting in Kate pulling her husband off the servant. Compare this empathetic Kate with her character earlier in the play, when she was more likely to be cursing and beating others. Curtis makes the point that Petruchio 'is more shrew than she' (4.1.63).

Petruchio complains about the standards of his servants. He sings 'Where is the life that late I led?' (4.1.111), reflecting on the fact that both Petruchio and Katherina have to adjust to their new life together. Servants enter with supper but Petruchio strikes them for imaginary offences. Kate defends them, feeling compelled by his excessive behaviour to be the reasonable half of the pair. Petruchio rejects the meal, throwing food and dishes back at the servants while Kate tries to calm him: 'I pray you, husband, be not so disquiet' (4.1.139). Petruchio suggests that, instead, they fast. The servant Peter accurately discerns that Petruchio 'kills her in her own humour' (4.1.151), which puns on Petruchio's reference to humoural theory (see page 9 of this guide). Petruchio makes Kate feel what it is like to be on the receiving end of her temper.

Petruchio takes Katherina to the bedroom but instead of them spending a romantic wedding night together, Petruchio, as Curtis recounts, gives Kate 'a sermon of continency' (4.1.154): that is, a lecture on self-restraint. Petruchio then enters and in a soliloquy reveals his strategy to the audience. He uses the analogy of falconry (training a falcon to do its master's bidding; a falcon is trained not to eat until its master gives permission, even if it is hungry). Having left Katherina hungry, Petruchio also intends to disrupt her sleep: 'And thus I'll curb her mad and headstrong humour' (4.1.180). Petruchio also directs a rhetorical statement at the audience, challenging them to suggest a better way 'to tame a shrew' (4.1.181). Although Katherina may have been perceived as unreasonable in the earlier parts of the play, modern audiences are likely to feel uncomfortable about Petruchio's cruel methods.

4.2 Summary: *Tranio (as Lucentio) purports to end his pursuit of Bianca after Hortensio shows him 'Cambio' (Lucentio) with Bianca. Hortensio decides to marry a wealthy widow instead, training her according to the principles of Petruchio's 'taming-school'. Tranio cons a merchant from Mantua to pretend to be Lucentio's father Vincentio.*

Outside Baptista's house, Tranio and Hortensio become another onstage audience as Hortensio informs Tranio (as Lucentio) of his discovery that Bianca favours 'Cambio' (Lucentio). They observe Bianca and Lucentio together as Lucentio is reading Ovid's *The Art of Love*. Tranio pretends to be shocked and complains of 'unconstant womankind!' (4.2.14), while in fact he is no doubt pleased at his master's success. Hortensio reveals his disguise to Tranio and that he is in fact a gentleman, not a lowborn tutor. Tranio claims he will now abandon his suit and Hortensio does likewise. There is dramatic irony in that the audience, unlike Hortensio, is aware of Tranio and Lucentio's collusion. Hortensio instead proposes to woo a wealthy widow who loves him. After Hortensio exits, Tranio tells Lucentio and Bianca of Hortensio's plans to follow the 'taming-school' of Petruchio (4.2.54, 55). Biondello announces that he has found a suitable old man to pretend to be Lucentio's father; Tranio tells the unsuspecting Merchant that anyone arriving from Mantua faces death in Padua but that he will help him if the Merchant agrees to disguise himself as 'Vincentio' of Pisa, Lucentio's father. The Merchant readily agrees.

4.3 Summary: *Katherina is deprived of food and fine clothing before Petruchio proposes they visit her family. He compels her to agree with his contrary perspective of the world.*

Katherina tries to persuade Grumio to get her some food but he follows his master's cruelty, finding excuses, based on humoural theory, for not bringing particular dishes. In frustration, Katherina beats Grumio. Petruchio and Hortensio enter with meat but Petruchio continues to deny any to Kate. Petruchio then proposes that Kate will be finely dressed; however, he pretends that the offerings from the tailor and haberdasher are substandard and again deprives her. Katherina, in a powerful protest against the silencing of women, proclaims her right to speak (4.3.73–80). Petruchio in response equates Kate's protest with a claim that she doesn't like the cap, thus implying that if she speaks out she will not receive the clothing. Likewise with the gown, Petruchio rails against the tailor, although he quietly arranges for Hortensio to pay the tailor, thus indicating that his act is just a strategy to tame Kate. Petruchio claims his own reality – 'It shall be what o'clock I say it is' (4.3.189) – and compels Kate to comply.

Key point

In 4.3, after denying Katherina fine clothes and proposing that they visit her father's house in their ordinary clothes, Petruchio philosophises that ''tis the mind that makes the body rich' and that 'honour peereth in the meanest habit' (4.3.166, 168) – that it is substance over appearance that is important. Could this be a clue to Katherina that his surface behaviour is not his true self? In their journey back to her family, Kate learns to play Petruchio's contrary games that create a gap between language and reality. This will be important for how we interpret Kate's famous speech in the final scene.

4.4 Summary: *Tranio takes 'Vincentio' (the Merchant) to Baptista, who agrees to the wedding between 'Lucentio' and Bianca.*

Tranio and the Merchant, disguised as Vincentio, arrive at Baptista's house and Tranio instructs Biondello to maintain the pretence. Baptista agrees that Lucentio may have Bianca if 'Vincentio' provides a sufficient dowry. Ironically, he instructs 'Cambio' (Lucentio) to tell Bianca the news. Biondello neatly sums up the situation when he says that Baptista is 'talking with the deceiving father of a deceitful son' (4.4.80–1). Foreshadowing Lucentio taking Bianca away for a secret marriage, Biondello comically comments, 'I knew a wench married in an afternoon as she went to the garden for parsley to stuff a rabbit' (4.5.95–6).

4.5 Summary: *On the road back to Padua, Kate learns to agree with Petruchio's nonsensical statements and to treat it as a game. They encounter the real Vincentio heading to Padua to see his son Lucentio, and Petruchio tells him of his son's marriage.*

Petruchio continues with his contrary ways on the journey back to Padua – while he claims that the moon shines, Katherina points out that it is the sun. Hortensio advises Kate to just agree with Petruchio so that they can go: 'Say as he says, or we shall never go' (4.5.11). Kate agrees to go along with whatever nonsense Petruchio claims: 'Henceforth I vow it shall be so for me' (4.5.15), which is a turning point in their relationship. The fact that the following line is a shared line – Petruchio: 'I say it is the moon';

Katherina: 'I know it is the moon' (4.5.16) – shows that they are now playing the same game, and Hortensio says in an aside that Petruchio has won the battle of wills: 'The field is won' (4.5.23).

The real Vincentio enters and, when Petruchio describes him as a 'gentlewoman' (4.5.29), Kate continues the jest enthusiastically, calling Vincentio a 'young budding virgin' (4.5.37). When Petruchio quickly changes tack, saying, 'This is a man' (4.5.43), Kate follows his cue. Vincentio comments on this 'strange encounter' with the pair that has 'much amazed' him (4.5.54) and tells them he is heading to Padua to see his son Lucentio. Petruchio seems to already know that Lucentio and Bianca are married. Vincentio, understandably, doubts whether Petruchio is telling the truth: 'But is this true, or is it else your pleasure, / Like pleasant travellers, to break a jest / Upon the company you overtake?' (4.5.71–3). Hortensio assures him of the truth and, after the others exit, he expresses in a half-rhyming couplet (froward/untoward 4.5.78–9) how Petruchio has taught him to tame his future wife.

Key vocabulary

jades (4.1.1): worn out horses

horn (4.1.20): cuckold's horn; sign of husband whose wife is unfaithful

cony-catching (4.1.30): trickery (from rabbit-hunting)

fustian (4.1.33): coarse cloth

Jacks; Jills (4.1.34, 35): male and female servants; drinking cups

Imprimis (4.1.48): to begin

bemoiled (4.1.56): covered with mud

Cock's (4.1.89): God's

spaniel Troilus (4.1.121): in folktales of taming a shrew, the husband intimidates his wife by punishing his dog

trenchers (4.1.136): wooden plates

man my haggard (4.1.164): tame or train my hawk (a bird from the wild, not captivity) *cullion* (4.2.20): lower-class fellow

ancient angel (4.2.61): old man; answer to my prayer; gold coin

marcantant (4.2.63): merchant

amort (4.3.36): depressed

farthingales (4.3.56): hooped skirts

porringer (4.3.64): small basin

custard-coffin (4.3.82): pastry case

bemete (4.3.111): measure, beat

Pegasus (4.4.5): winged horse from mythology (here the name of an inn)

affied (4.4.49): betrothed

scrivener (4.4.59): notary

cum … solum (4.4.89–90): with exclusive rights to father children

rush-candle (4.5.14): candle that gives a feeble light

Q Analyse Petruchio's contrary statements on the journey back to visit the Minola household. What is the effect of this game he plays?

Q In 4.4 the servant Biondello speaks a Latin phrase; what is ironic about this?

Act 5

5.1 Summary: *Lucentio and Bianca steal away for their secret wedding. Meanwhile, the real Vincentio confronts the Merchant (as Vincentio). Lucentio and Bianca return after the ceremony to the anger of their fathers. Petruchio manages to obtain a kiss from Katherina.*

Lucentio appears as himself with Bianca, and Biondello tells them that the priest is ready so the couple exit for their secret wedding. In a moment of dramatic irony, Gremio wonders why 'Cambio' the tutor has not appeared. The Merchant, as Vincentio, appears at a window, creating confusion when the real Vincentio asks to speak to his son and the Merchant insists that he is Vincentio. The Merchant claims that it is the real Vincentio who is trying to play a trick. Vincentio challenges Biondello who pretends not to know him, whereupon Vincentio beats him. Petruchio and Katherina watch on – a rare moment when they are not the centre of attention. Tranio maintains the pretence, calling Vincentio a madman, while Vincentio retorts that Tranio's father is 'a sail-maker in Bergamo' (5.1.60). Vincentio, alarmed, suspects that Tranio has murdered his son.

Lucentio, Bianca and Biondello return, and Tranio and the Merchant make a hasty exit. Lucentio and Bianca kneel and ask forgiveness of their fathers, revealing the deceit – 'Cambio is changed into Lucentio' (5.1.97) – and their secret marriage. Baptista is furious that Lucentio married Bianca without asking for her father's consent; he has had to cope with another unconventional wedding. Note how Vincentio's and Baptista's speech mode shifts from verse to prose in their anger.

Petruchio and Katherina are left alone on the street and Petruchio demands a kiss. At first, she hesitates, since it's in a public street, but then, as Petruchio prepares to leave, she consents and calls him 'love' (5.1.123). Note the repetition of 'What' by the pair (5.1.117–18), the use of anaphora underlining the connection between them.

5.2 Summary: *Katherina and the Widow, Hortensio's new wife, clash over the Widow's assertion that Petruchio is troubled with a shrew. Petruchio proposes a bet among the men to see whose wife will obediently come when called. To everyone's amazement, Kate appears, unlike the other wives, and furthermore gives an accomplished rhetorical speech on wifely obedience.*

Lucentio's comment that 'At last, though long, our jarring notes agree, / And time it is when raging war is done' (5.2.1–2) reflects broadly on the states of the pairs of lovers. With the appearance of the Widow, Hortensio's new wife, and Petruchio's suggestion that Hortensio may be afraid of her, there is the potential for a new 'shrew' figure. The Widow misunderstands Petruchio and claims she is not afraid of Hortensio. Petruchio corrects her and the Widow makes an observation about how perspective depends on the circumstances of the viewer; she quotes a proverb: 'He that is giddy thinks the world turns around' (5.2.20). When Katherina questions the Widow, the latter asserts that Petruchio is 'troubled with a shrew' (5.2.28) and thus assumes that all husbands are likewise afflicted. Katherina is offended and she and the Widow prepare to argue, encouraged by Petruchio and Hortensio, Petruchio willing to bet on his wife winning the fight. Baptista comments to Gremio on 'these quick-witted folks' (5.2.38), acknowledging the education that underpins these various verbal conflicts. Even Bianca joins in the verbal jousting, showing her ability and willingness to speak out, like her sister.

After the women exit, the male characters draw on the language of hunting. Tranio asserts that Kate is still getting the better of Petruchio so Petruchio proposes a bet: the winner will be the husband whose wife comes first when sent for. They agree on a hundred crowns. Neither Bianca nor the Widow comes at her husband's command. Petruchio then sends for Kate who promptly enters, to everyone's astonishment. Petruchio directs Kate to bring the other wives in (and to beat them if they refuse). Hortensio wonders what this foreshadows and Petruchio claims that it signals future marital happiness: 'peace it bodes, and love, and quiet life' (5.2.108).

Baptista is so amazed at the transformation of his daughter that he offers to increase the dowry paid to Petruchio. Petruchio presses the point further, telling Kate to take off her cap and throw it underfoot, which she does. The Widow and Bianca call Katherina's submission 'silly' and 'foolish duty' (5.2.124, 125). Petruchio tells Katherina to tell the other women what duty they owe to their husbands. In her speech, she claims that the husband is 'thy lord, thy king, thy governor' (5.2.138), an idea common in the early modern period but contrary to today's ideas about marriage. She uses various literary techniques and shows off her rhetorical skill, that is, her ability to persuade. The object of the speech is to persuade the other women, and its power is all the more impressive since it is highly likely that Kate does not really believe these ideas. Petruchio, well pleased with Kate's performance and display of rhetorical skill, proposes that they go to bed, leaving the others dumbfounded at the transformation of 'a curst shrew' (5.2.188).

Key point

Katherina's speech in the final scene has been controversial throughout the play's history, creating a dilemma for directors and actors. Yet the very polished nature of the speech, its verbal skill and use of rhetorical techniques, signal it as a type of performance. This therefore alters how we read Kate's 'submission'. Also note the caveat that Kate suggests women be obedient to their husband's 'honest will' (5.2.158) – where the husband's request is honourable and legitimate – leaving open the possibility of resisting where the husband's request is unreasonable. There is also a clue to the performative nature of the speech when Kate says: 'Our strength as weak, our weakness past compare, / That seeming to be most which we indeed least are' (5.2.174–5). The use of 'seeming' points to the gap between surface appearances and truth.

Key vocabulary

crack-hemp (5.1.36): villain who deserves hanging

doublet (5.1.52): close-fitting jacket

copatain (5.1.53): dome-shaped

holidame (5.2.99): Virgin Mary; holy dame

go thy ways (5.2.181): well done

sped (5.2.185): done for

Q What changes in Bianca's character are revealed after she is married?

Q To what extent does the play suggest that being a shrew is a type of role that women, and even men, can take on, as opposed to being an intrinsic part of someone's personality? Justify your answer with evidence from the play.

CHARACTERS & RELATIONSHIPS

In the medieval theatre that predated Shakespeare, characters had less depth and were generally embodiments of abstract ideas (such as vice) or figures known to the audience from biblical stories or historical tales. They fulfilled certain roles and functions in a play, making it less important to provide personal detail, since they were subservient to the overall structure. Shakespeare is credited with being among the first playwrights to give characters a greater interiority, giving us more information about what they think and feel, and allowing us to construct psychological profiles for them. This depth is not provided uniformly across the play; we learn more about some characters than others. There is also often a complexity to Shakespeare's characters that makes us respond to them as plausible people rather than types (characters who represent certain ideas or embody particular human characteristics). Very few of Shakespeare's characters can be reduced to a simple stereotype; there are often flaws in his heroes and elements of virtue in his villains.

Katherina

Key quotes

'Her only fault – and that is faults enough –
Is that she is intolerable curst,
And shrewd and froward so beyond all measure
That, were my state far worser than it is,
I would not wed her for a mine of gold!' (Hortensio, 1.2.84–8)
'"Katherine the curst"!
A title for a maid of all titles the worst.' (Grumio, 1.2.123–4)

Katherina, the 'shrew', is feisty, outspoken and resistant. She repels most of the male figures around her, criticised for her 'loud alarums' (1.1.123) and known for her 'scolding tongue' (1.2.96). Gremio says that being married to her would be like being publicly whipped every day (1.1.127).

Kate is highly intelligent and witty, quick with verbal insults that display her education. In Petruchio she meets her match: someone who is equally intelligent and quick with insults.

Katherina clears a physical and mental space around her through her 'shrewish' behaviour, yet the result of pushing others away is a degree of loneliness. We sense that there is hurt beneath Katherina's actions, as a result of both her father's attitude towards her, and her own jealousy of Bianca. Her complaint to Baptista in 2.1 reveals her emotions: 'She is your treasure, she must have a husband. / I must dance barefoot on her wedding day' (2.1.32–3). Furthermore, her talk of weddings suggests that, despite Katherina's hostility to men, part of her would also like to be married.

Thus paradoxically, although Katherina on one level rejects Petruchio's advances, she is also, at the same time, taken aback by his attentions and flattery. She is offended when he comes late to the wedding in unsuitable clothes and this suggests that to some degree, despite her resistance to gendered expectations, nevertheless she cares about and wants to participate in normal social rituals and conventions: to have a wedding where the groom turns up on time and is wearing suitable clothes. Thus, as much as Kate wants to pull away from her family and society, part of her also wants to belong.

In the scene of the bet (5.2), Kate performs the role of the dutiful wife. To what extent is this a choice? When she lived at home, Kate's father did not withhold food, even when she had tantrums. Now that she is married to Petruchio, she is vulnerable as she is subject to his rules, and his behaviour makes it clear that unless she tries to appease him, she will not be fed or provided for. Petruchio does not frame his actions as a form of withholding; rather, he frames them as arising from a concern that the food is not good enough, a position that he takes to an extreme. By matching Kate's earlier extreme behaviour, he implicitly invites her to become more moderate, to find a happy medium. By the final scene, Kate has indeed come to a moderate position and reconciled herself to having an amicable relationship with her new husband.

Although Kate is arguably conforming to society's expected role for a wife, in this scene she still acts in opposition to how the other women do (they choose at this moment to disobey their husbands). Thus, Kate continues to set herself apart, and to be a nonconforming individual, like Petruchio. Furthermore, by playing her part, and choosing to comply with her husband's wishes, Kate shows it to be a choice, not a compulsion; the other wives choose differently. Kate gives Petruchio the courtesy of her compliance at this moment, so he can win the bet, thus receiving her husband's gratitude, and opening up the potential for a relationship of mutual trust.

Key point

Is Kate 'tamed'? Every production of *The Taming of the Shrew* must decide how they will shape the resolution of the play. Through gestures, facial expressions, and movement, actors and directors have freedom to interpret the play text. Is Kate's spirit broken by Petruchio's coercive control? Or does she choose to enter into his game of contrariness, knowing that he is also performing and that, with their equal intelligence and wit, they have the potential for a rewarding relationship?

Petruchio

Key quotes

'Antonio my father is deceased
And I have thrust myself into this maze,
Happily to wive and thrive as best I may.
Crowns in my purse I have, and goods at home,
And so am come abroad to see the world.' (1.2.51–5)
'I come to wive it wealthily in Padua;
If wealthily, then happily in Padua.' (1.2.72–3)
'… kiss me, Kate …' (2.1.313)

Petruchio has come from Verona to Padua to visit friends, particularly his good friend Hortensio. He has also come with the aim of finding a wife, although part of his initial motivation to woo Katherina is his friendship with Hortensio, who is pursuing Bianca and would benefit from Katherina being married. Like most early modern suitors, Petruchio is equally motivated by financial gain; marriage in the period often resembled a financial transaction. By marrying Katherina, he will receive a significant dowry from her father Baptista Minola.

Like Katherina, Petruchio resists conforming to society's expectations. Whereas other suitors run a mile from the difficult Katherina, Petruchio sees her as a challenge, relishing this rather than trying to take the easier option of Bianca. Petruchio is not concerned about public appearances, and he demonstrates to Katherina that he too can defy society. He dresses in ridiculous clothes for his wedding and pretends to be a volatile and irrational husband. In this, he plays a role in order to assert *himself* as the difficult, contrary partner in the marriage, leaving Katherina bewildered and demoralised. Yet by behaving against the norms of society, Petruchio signals his parallels to Kate.

Petruchio is like Katherina in several ways; like her, he is feisty and quick to threaten physical violence. Katherina is physically and verbally violent to several other characters early in the play, and likewise Petruchio threatens his servant Grumio (1.2.12) and wrings him by the ears, and is violent towards his servants after the wedding. Like Katherina, Petruchio is intelligent and witty, able to match her insults in their bouts of verbal sparring. While initially Petruchio likely sees Katherina only as a financial proposition and a challenge, in the course of their wooing and marriage their similarities and suitability become evident, creating the potential for mutual attraction to emerge in parallel to their sparring.

Although Petruchio acts in cruel ways towards Kate, and plays the eccentric husband, we sense that he is not innately cruel, and that his actions are a type of performance intended to counter Kate's hostility and neutralise her antipathy towards him. Even though a modern audience may not agree with his methods, we might interpret the similarities and rapport between Petruchio and Kate as suggesting their marriage will settle down and perhaps have a better chance of becoming a mutually satisfactory relationship than other more conventional pairings.

Key point

Petruchio's treatment of Katherina after their wedding, in depriving her of food and sleep and in dominating and controlling her, unsettles us as contemporary readers and audiences. While early modern society was more accustomed to seeing women treated as property, we perceive Petruchio's behaviour as domestic violence, and this challenges our responses to him.

Lucentio

Key quotes

'Tranio, I burn! I pine, I perish, Tranio,
If I achieve not this young modest girl.' (1.1.146–7)
'Cambio is changed into Lucentio.' (Bianca, 5.1.97)

Lucentio, like Petruchio, has arrived in Padua as an eager scholar and a young man ready to seek his fortunes. He quickly falls in love with Bianca Minola, after only briefly seeing her and hearing her say very little. His conventional language and melodramatic response to Bianca suggest a lack of depth to his feelings; since he has only seen her external appearance and knows nothing of her as a person, the attachment is superficial.

Lucentio faces several challenges in that Bianca is not allowed to marry before Katherina, and already has several suitors pursuing her. Lucentio proves himself resourceful and disguises himself as Cambio (an Italian word meaning an exchange or change) to gain access to Bianca. When his servant Tranio (pretending to be Lucentio) successfully outbids Gremio for Bianca's hand on behalf of Lucentio, Lucentio is faced with a new challenge of producing a wealthy father. Ultimately Lucentio is successful in winning Bianca, but by marrying her in secret he risks the wrath of her father. He also risks the wrath of his own father Vincentio, particularly once the deceit involving the Merchant is revealed. However, by the end of the play, all parties appear to be reconciled.

Bianca

Key quotes

'Sir, to your pleasure humbly I subscribe.
My books and instruments shall be my company ...' (1.1.81–2)

Hortensio: Did you yet ever see Baptista's daughter?
Tranio: No, sir, but hear I do that he hath two,
The one as famous for a scolding tongue
As is the other for beauteous modesty. (1.2.245–8)

Bianca appears to be everything Katherina is not. Compliant, submissive and obedient to her father, Bianca conforms to early modern society's ideas of the perfect woman and wife. For example, when Baptista tells her to go into the house, she immediately obeys (1.1.75–81). Unsurprisingly, she has many suitors. Bianca's role as favourite daughter makes Katherina jealous and angry; she sees Bianca as a 'pretty peat' (1.1.78), a spoilt child, and demonstrates her feelings by bullying Bianca in a scene of physical violence that foreshadows Petruchio's bullying of Katherina. The conventions of society force Katherina and Bianca into a bad daughter / good daughter binary. Baptista contributes to this paradigm, failing to give Katherina the love and attention she needs and clearly favouring one daughter over the other: 'And so farewell. Katherina, you may stay, / For I have more to commune with Bianca' (1.1.100–1). Yet at the end of the play there are signs that Bianca may have learned something from Katherina.

Key point

Lucentio is initially attracted to Bianca because she conforms to the expectations of women; he comments on her 'silence' and 'mild behaviour' (1.1.70, 71). Given this, it may seem likely that Lucentio and Bianca's marriage will not be as intellectually fulfilling as Katherina and Petruchio's. However, after she is married, Bianca joins in a conversation of verbal jousting (5.2.40–8) and, during the final scene, in the bet, she resists obeying Lucentio's demand to attend him. Thus, the sisters shift roles and Bianca becomes (at least in this scene) the assertive, contrary wife. Perhaps she has learned something from her sister?

The minor characters

Christopher Sly is the key figure of the frame narrative. A drunken tinker, he is thrown out of a tavern, passes out drunk, then, upon waking, finds himself the subject of a trick by a Lord and Bartholomew, his page. Sly is gullible and easily seduced by the fantasy of living an upper-class life.

Baptista Minola is the father of two very different daughters. Aware that he is unlikely to find a suitor for his difficult eldest daughter Katherina, he refuses Bianca permission to marry until Katherina does. This does not help the conflict between the sisters. Baptista's favouring of Bianca contributes to Katherina's hurt, which further fuels her anger and violent outbursts.

Gremio and **Hortensio** compete for Bianca's hand. Gremio is a stock character indebted to the *commedia dell'arte* tradition. As a rich, foolish old man, he believes he can buy Bianca; however, the large age difference between them makes him an unappealing prospect for her, and a laughing-stock to the audience. Hortensio, like Lucentio, adopts a disguise ('Litio'), pretending to be a music tutor to gain access to Bianca, but eventually he marries a **Widow**.

A range of other minor characters helps to create the world of the play. **Tranio** is Lucentio's quick-witted servant who plays a key role by pretending to be Lucentio (while Lucentio is busy pretending to be Cambio). **Grumio** is Petruchio's personal servant (not to be confused with **Gremio**, the rich old suitor). while **Biondello** is Lucentio's second servant. Other minor characters are **Vincentio**, the father of Lucentio, and a **Merchant**, who pretends to be Vincentio.

THEMES, IDEAS & VALUES

The construction of gender

Key quotes

Hortensio: No mates for you
Unless you were of gentler, milder mould. (1.1.59–60)
Tranio: That wench is stark mad, or wonderful froward. (1.1.69)
Lucentio: But in the other's silence do I see
Maid's mild behaviour and sobriety. (1.1.70–1)

Contemporary theorists in literary and cultural studies have demonstrated the ways in which gender is a construction. Society shapes the expected behaviours and definitions of gender (distinct from biological sex), and these have shifted throughout history. In the modern era we are aware that there are more than two genders and that to think in terms of strict binaries is problematic, and that gender and sexuality are more usefully thought of as a continuum, encompassing a spectrum of identities and behaviours. However, in the early modern period, gender was more strictly defined and regimented. Individuals whose behaviour crossed the boundaries of what was deemed feminine or masculine were often thought of as a threat or monstrous, deserving of punishment and control by society. An outspoken woman was sometimes considered a masculine woman; speaking out was transgressive because it crossed gender boundaries. Gremio suggests that Katherina should suffer 'penance' because of 'her tongue' (1.1.89).

In the early modern period, a woman was expected to be silent, chaste and obedient. This reflected masculine anxieties about the potential power of women and thus the need to control them by patrolling the borders of their bodies and their behaviour. In the first part of the Induction, the Lord advises Bartholomew how to be a dutiful wife, which introduces in a comic way a theme of the main play. Humour is created when the Lord instructs Bartholomew to be 'humble', 'show her duty', and place a 'declining head into his bosom' (Induction 1.112, 113, 115). These instructions will be in stark contrast to the behaviour of Katherina. Yet Bartholomew, as a male character playing a female role, is a type of masculine woman, thus in one way a mirror to Katherina (herself a female character performed by a male actor in Shakespeare's time).

Katherina is often described in negative ways because of her outspoken nature. For example, Gremio describes her as a 'fiend of hell' (1.1.88) and tells her to 'go to the devil's dam!' (1.1.105), suggesting she is demonic. Voice was often linked with sexual promiscuity; thus, a woman's volubility was potentially a sign of a lack of chastity. Speaking out is also about claiming autonomy, so an outspoken woman was a threat to masculine attempts to control her. Katherina's resistance against her society's male-dominated power includes verbally and physically assaulting those around her, and expressing her anger and defiance through insults and contrary behaviour.

The play presents compliance (or non-compliance) with gender norms in moral terms. Kate is categorised as bad because she refuses to comply with society's expectations. Bianca's mildness and silence are equated with goodness – her father describes her as 'good Bianca' (1.1.75–6). The private, domestic sphere was associated with women while the public space of the street was dominated by men. While Baptista instructs Bianca to return to the house, in contrast he tells Katherina 'you may stay' (1.1.100), which links the outspoken woman with the public space of the streets. Although the two instructions are different, the same assumption underpins them both: Baptista is entitled to direct their movements. Yet Katherina challenges this assumption: 'Why, and I trust I may go too, may I not? / What, shall I be appointed hours as though, belike, / I knew not what to take and what to leave? Ha!' (1.1.102–4). She asserts her right to make her own decisions.

Notice the type of language that is used to refer to women. Grumio, in emphasising Petruchio's focus on a rich wife, says that it doesn't matter whether Petruchio is married to a 'puppet' or an 'aglet-baby' (1.2.75), characterising the woman as an object and suggesting that the control husbands have over wives is like that of puppeteers over their puppets. Petruchio imagines his prospective wife as a ship: 'For I will board her though she chide as loud / As thunder when the clouds in autumn crack' (1.2.91–2).

Women were thought of as property belonging to men. When Hortensio describes a potential husband for Katherina who 'would take her with all faults' (1.1.124), he uses a phrase common in the context of a cattle market, suggesting that women are, like livestock, property to be bought, and that Kate is faulty stock to be disposed of. Even though Bianca is more attractive to the men around her, she is still thought of as property. When Hortensio says 'He that runs fastest gets the ring' (1.1.132–3), 'ring' means the wedding band, but was also a bawdy term for female genitalia. So, the word reduces Bianca to a sexual body part, objectifying her.

After the wedding, Petruchio gives a speech that reflects common attitudes towards women in the period:

> I will be master of what is mine own.
> She is my goods, my chattels; she is my house,
> My household-stuff, my field, my barn,
> My horse, my ox, my ass, my anything,
> And here she stands. (3.2.218–22)

These ideas are completely opposed to modern attitudes towards women. At the same time, Petruchio's exaggeration, taking the idea to extremes, suggests that he may not seriously believe this idea. Also indicative that Petruchio is only performing is the humour of his mock-chivalric pretence that the wedding party is threatening to take Kate away and that he will protect her.

Men were also subject to constructions of gender. Just as women were thought of as property belonging to men, men were expected to keep control of that property. Thus, a man who could not control his wife was thought of as emasculated, as not meeting society's expectations.

Petruchio is thus subject to the gendered expectation of being able to control his wife. His cruel actions in 'taming' Katherina need to be read in this context. However, Petruchio also demonstrates that he is willing to resist societal expectations. Despite the unsettling wooing process, there is the potential for them ultimately to have a relatively equitable relationship, each respecting the other.

Key point

Shakespeare creates dramatic interest by constructing a character in Katherina who defies the conventions of gender. Does this make Shakespeare a protofeminist (presenting feminist ideas before the feminist movement began)? Or are the conventions of gender challenged only in order to confirm the norm, with her taming? The play thus raises an interesting debate.

Disguise

Key quotes

'Thou shalt be master, Tranio, in my stead;
Keep house and port and servants as I should.
I will some other be – some Florentine,
Some Neapolitan or meaner man of Pisa.' (Lucentio, 1.1.193–6)

'Tranio is changed into Lucentio.' (Lucentio, 1.1.227)

'Now shall my friend Petruchio do me grace
And offer me disguised in sober robes
To old Baptista as a schoolmaster
Well seen in music, to instruct Bianca,
That so I may by this device at least
Have leave and leisure to make love to her
And unsuspected court her by herself.' (Hortensio, 1.2.125–31)

Disguise is a common device used by Shakespeare in his comedies and is a key theme throughout *Shrew*. It can be used to swap class status; for example, in the frame narrative, the Lord pretends Sly is a lord, which is mirrored in the inset play when Tranio, a servant, is disguised as Lucentio, his master. Two characters use disguise in order to woo Bianca – Lucentio disguises himself as the schoolmaster Cambio (an Italian word meaning exchange), and Hortensio disguises himself as Litio, a music tutor.

Clothes are a key method of creating disguise. Clothing in the early modern period was a sign of status and there were strict laws governing who could wear what kinds of clothing and materials. When Lucentio and Tranio swap roles and status, their different clothes, as master and servant, are enough in theory to complete the disguise. There was no elaborate scenery on Shakespeare's stage and only minimal props, so costumes were a key element in creating dramatic visual interest onstage and could be used for comic effect, creating identity and exploring themes of disguise. Some disguises lead to complications, offering the potential for dramatic comedy. For example, Tranio, pretending to be Lucentio, produces Lucentio's 'father' Vincentio, who is the Merchant in disguise. This causes problems (and creates humour) when the real Vincentio arrives.

The theme of disguise can be extended to role-playing generally. Is being a shrew a particular role that Katherina plays in order to assert her independence in a system that treats women as mere property? Petruchio, as part of his taming strategy, also performs the role of a shrew, to create a mirror for her behaviour. Arguably, the submissive wife is just as much a role and Katherina plays that role to help Petruchio win a bet in the final scene.

Key point

Sly being elevated to a lord as a joke, and Lucentio and Tranio, as master and servant, swapping clothes and status, both recall festive rituals in England in which a lower-class figure would be temporarily elevated for a day as a 'Lord of Misrule' and a source of comedy. Such rituals functioned as a pressure valve for society, allowing the common people to enjoy the fantasy of power, while also arguably affirming the status quo of a strict hierarchical system in which ordinary people had little power.

Money and property

Key quotes

'Why, nothing comes amiss, so money comes withal.' (Grumio, 1.2.77–8)
'Thou know'st not gold's effect.' (Petruchio, 1.2.89)

Money and ideas about property underlie many of the relationships and interactions in the play. Petruchio has arrived in Padua because he is now wealthy and is looking to marry. At the same time, Baptista is looking to offload his daughters. A dowry was a way that a father could pay to relieve himself of the burden of having to support his daughters. The dowry then created a financial incentive for a husband to take on a wife as his property. Thus, the marriage process was a transactional exchange: money for a woman.

Petruchio's primary motivation for marriage is money; in fact he claims that he does not care what kind of wife he marries, so long as she is wealthy: 'wealth is burden of my wooing dance' (1.2.65). He responds to Hortensio's warning about Kate by emphasising the power of money. When Petruchio discusses marriage with Baptista in 2.1, the discussion is centred on money: what Petruchio will receive as dowry, and what he has to offer to support Katherina.

At moments in the play, there is little difference between women and property; for example, Hortensio describes Bianca as 'my treasure' in Baptista's 'keep' and 'the jewel of my life' in Baptista's 'hold' (1.2.112, 113). The suitors seeking Bianca's hand in marriage compete by listing evidence of their wealth. That is, Baptista does not ask Bianca who she loves and would like to marry. Instead, he conducts a type of auction. Gremio, the rich old man, has the advantage here and he catalogues everything he has. Tranio, as 'Lucentio', has to match this and offer more, which he manages to do by stretching the truth.

The business of marriage in the early modern period also involved spending money and displaying wealth. Petruchio, upon becoming engaged to Katherina, sets off to purchase wedding clothes and other items. Meanwhile, Baptista likens his position to that of a merchant undertaking a risky venture – 'a desperate mart' (2.1.316). The language of trade underlines the equating of women with property. Both Baptista and Petruchio see the marriage as a business transaction; Tranio describes Katherina as a 'commodity' (2.1.317), and compares her to a ship that will either 'bring you gain' or 'perish on the seas' (2.1.318).

Key point

Shakespeare's society was in the process of shifting from one based on feudal values – in which the ties between people were based on reciprocal relationships of rights and duties – to a protocapitalist society in which money and property were the basis of transactions. Shakespeare and his contemporaries explored onstage the blurred boundaries between people and property. The idea of women as objects of exchange conflicts with our contemporary values; we see women as subjects, not objects. In Katherina's hostile objections to such early modern society norms, we can see the beginnings of ideas that would ultimately result, in later ages, in recognition of the rights of women.

Metatheatre

Key quotes

'Therefore they thought it good you hear a play ...' (Servant, Induction 2.129)
'And gaze your fill.' (Tranio, 1.1.73)

In *The Taming of the Shrew*, there are multiple layers through which Shakespeare draws our attention to performance and spectatorship, the essence of theatre. Firstly, the frame narrative with Sly casts the main part of *The Taming of the Shrew* as a play-within-a-play. A term for this is 'metatheatre': theatre that draws attention to its own nature. Other spectators are created at various points in the play, helping to remind the audience that what they are watching is a performance, not reality. For example, in 1.1, shortly after Lucentio and Tranio arrive in Padua, they stand aside to watch the Minola family arriving, thus creating an additional audience.

There are also various performances by different characters – some in disguise – that are metatheatrical. When Bartholomew dresses as a woman in the Induction scene, this recalls the practice in Shakespeare's theatre of boys playing female parts. Bartholomew has to act as a noble lady, based on what he has 'observed in noble ladies' (Induction 1.107). Lucentio and Hortensio play the role of scholars in order to secretly woo Bianca. Petruchio performs the role of the eccentric suitor and husband to match Katherina's behaviour.

Gender can also be seen as the performance of a role. Kate initially rejects the role expected of her by society, that of the compliant, submissive woman. However, in the final scene she chooses to play that role as a gesture of goodwill towards her husband. Bianca and other wives choose not to play the role at that time. The effect of this is to make gendered behaviour a type of performance, reminding us of the role of theatre in expressing different facets of human nature and testing ideas. All of these types of roles and performances invite us to reflect on the nature of theatre itself.

Key point

The prefix 'meta' is a useful term to know for literary analysis. We can use it where a text is drawing attention to its own nature and mechanisms, as with the play-within-a-play here. You can also use 'meta' in other contexts, for example 'metafilmic' when a film draws attention to aspects of the medium of film; or 'metafictional', when a novel has a third-person narrator speak directly to us as readers, thus inviting us to step back and reflect on the process of creating fiction itself.

Education

Key quotes

'To see fair Padua, nursery of arts,
I am arrived for fruitful Lombardy,
The pleasant garden of great Italy,
...
Here let us breathe and haply institute
A course of learning and ingenious studies.' (Lucentio, 1.1.2–9)

'No profit grows where is no pleasure tane:
In brief, sir, study what you most affect.' (Tranio, 1.1.39–40)

'O this learning, what a thing it is!' (Gremio, 1.2.153)

Education is a key theme in *The Taming of the Shrew*. Padua is an old university town, with a university dating back to the thirteenth century; Lucentio describes it as a 'nursery of arts' (1.1.2). In the early modern period, there was a revival of interest in the culture of ancient Greece and Rome. The works of ancient authors were translated and disseminated, forming an important part of the curriculum for those fortunate enough to receive an education. When the suitors present themselves to Baptista in 2.1, Gremio claims 'Cambio' has knowledge of Greek and Latin, and 'Lucentio' presents a gift of Greek and Latin books for Bianca. Shakespeare's schooling in Stratford included the study of Latin and of classical authors such as Ovid and Aristotle, reflected in references in his plays.

When Lucentio and Tranio discuss different approaches to education, Tranio refers to the Stoics: 'Let's be no stoics' (1.1.31), since he's concerned that his master Lucentio may take study too seriously. Stoicism is a philosophy that emphasises self-control and Stoics are in theory unmoved by external events; they aim to stay calm and maintain an equilibrium of mind. Tranio also refers to the study of 'rhetoric' (1.1.35), the art of persuasion, which Shakespeare would have learnt in grammar school. Other areas of study Tranio refers to are logic and metaphysics

(1.1.34, 37). Tranio displays his own learning when he wisely observes that scolding Lucentio for falling in love with Bianca will have little effect, and he quotes in Latin (1.1.153).

Petruchio and Hortensio speak briefly in Italian when they first meet, emphasising the Italian setting and evidencing Shakespeare's education. Even though Grumio is presumably Italian, he appears not to recognise Italian and thinks they are speaking Latin; this shows his lack of education but also imagines him as an English character, rather than Italian.

When Gremio consults the tutor Cambio (Lucentio in disguise) about the list of books he proposes for Bianca, he says, 'I'll have them very fairly bound' (1.2.139). In the early modern period, people bought books in loose-leaf form, with the printed pages unbound, and then arranged for their own preferred bindings to be made for the books. Gremio has chosen books on the theme of love for Lucentio to instruct Bianca in, unknowingly helping Lucentio. This is a moment of dramatic irony since the audience knows more than the foolish Gremio.

Education in the play is intertwined with love. Lucentio arrives in Padua with the aim of embarking on a course of studies, but he is quickly diverted into an education in love. The suitors use roles as scholars to gain access to Bianca, and also to woo her through knowledge. Lucentio and Hortensio compete through the lessons they offer her in music and philosophy; both subjects comprised part of a traditional education in the liberal arts. Gremio recognises the threat that Tranio (as Lucentio) represents with his witty way with words and display of learning, such as references to Leda's daughter (Helen of Troy) and Paris (1.2.237, 240), exclaiming, 'What, this gentleman will out-talk us all!' (1.2.241). This proves prophetic since it is Tranio's wit that will ultimately secure Bianca for his master Lucentio.

Katherina and Petruchio also undergo a process of education in dealing with each other. Petruchio behaves in a shrewish way to meet the challenges Katherina poses for any potential wooers, while Katherina learns to moderate her behaviour to deal with her seemingly irrational new husband. Hortensio sees Petruchio as the master of a type of 'taming-school' (4.2.54), as Tranio calls it, the principles of which Hortensio hopes to follow in taming his wealthy widow.

Key point

There were restrictions on the education of women in the early modern period, and it was generally only women from the upper class or the landed gentry who had access to any kind of formal learning, and that was primarily confined to the domestic sphere. Although Baptista's daughters are unable to attend a school or university, he wants them to gain knowledge and attributes that will help them in society and to attract husbands. He arranges tutors to instruct Bianca: 'for I know she taketh most delight / In music, instruments and poetry, / Schoolmasters will I keep within my house / Fit to instruct her youth' (1.1.92–5). Ironically, these lessons will provide Bianca's suitors with an opportunity to woo her.

DIFFERENT INTERPRETATIONS

Different interpretations arise from different responses to a text. Over time, a text will evoke a wide range of responses from its readers, who may come from various social or cultural groups and live in very different places and historical periods. Responses by critics and reviewers can be published in newspapers, journals and books, both online and in print. They can also be expressed in discussions among readers in the media, classrooms, book groups and so on.

While there is no single correct reading or interpretation of a text, it is important to understand that an interpretation is more than a personal opinion – it is the justification of a point of view on the text. To present an interpretation of a text based on your point of view, you must use a logical argument and support it with relevant evidence from the text.

The critics' viewpoints

Literary criticism, often referred to as 'secondary sources', is writing *about* a text, the 'primary source', and analyses, comments on and offers a particular interpretation of the primary text. Literary critics, in writing about a text, are entering into a dialogue with other critics and take into account the opinions of others. Since Shakespeare's work has been around for several centuries, there is a substantial amount of critical material about his plays and poetry. This can be daunting for students and critics alike; keep in mind that it is not possible for anyone to read and understand everything that is relevant to the play. Try to select a few articles or book sections that discuss an area of interest to you. Reading literary criticism should be enjoyable and will help you order your thoughts and shape your own ideas about the play. It can also open your eyes to aspects of the play that you had not previously noticed.

Different interpretations of the play are also created every time it is performed as a stage production or produced as a film. A particular production constitutes an interpretation because directors, script editors, cinematographers and others make choices such as to cut, add or rearrange lines and scenes. Choices are also made regarding costumes, sets, casting, props, music, sound and visual effects. Seeing performances and/or film adaptations of the play is an effective way of informing your subjective interpretations.

Often Shakespearean texts are also adapted into other forms or used as the basis for more modern tellings of the plot. For example, the 1948 musical *Kiss Me, Kate* (Bella and Samuel Spewack with Cole Porter) is an interpretation of *The Taming of the Shrew*, and the 1999 film *10 Things I Hate About You* (dir. Gil Junger) is a modernisation of the play.

Many scholarly editions of the play provide a valuable introduction and overview, considering themes, historical contexts and aspects of characterisation; they provide summaries of the different approaches taken by critics and look at stage and film histories. These can provide a useful starting point for determining which aspects of the play you wish to research. It is also useful to look at edited collections of essays on the play, which provide a range of different perspectives, rather than just one critic's viewpoint.

If you are new to Shakespeare, it is useful to start with some background information about his life, historical period and why he has proved to be such an enduring writer. Some excellent places to start are Jonathan Bate's *Soul of the Age* (2008); his earlier work *The Genius of Shakespeare* (1997); Stephen Greenblatt's *Will in the World: How Shakespeare Became Shakespeare* (2004); and Peter Ackroyd's *Shakespeare: The Biography* (2005). Also useful are *The Oxford Companion to Shakespeare* (Dobson et al. 2015), with plot summaries and valuable critical and stage histories on each of the plays, and *The Shakespeare Encyclopedia* (Driver et al. 2009), a good general introduction with historical images and contemporary stills from stage and film productions. *The New Cambridge Companion to Shakespeare* (De Grazia & Wells 2010) is also an invaluable resource with essays by various contributors on Shakespeare's life, what he read, his language, genres, aspects of gender, and the life of the theatre in Shakespeare's time.

In terms of approaching *The Taming of the Shrew* from the perspective of genre, valuable insights can be found in *The Cambridge Introduction to Shakespeare's Comedies* (Gay 2008), in which Penny Gay explores *Shrew* from the perspective of farce, and *The Cambridge Companion to Shakespearean Comedy* (Leggett 2001), for example in Chapter 8 where Edward Berry explores the theme of laughter and 'others' or outsiders. These will help you to think about aspects relevant to *Shrew* as well as issues common to all of Shakespeare's comedies.

In seeking an overview of the diverse issues that the play raises, two excellent starting places are Marjorie Garber's chapter on the play in her *Shakespeare After All* (2004), and Jean E Howard's introduction to the play in *The Norton Shakespeare* (2016). Another excellent overview is Margaret Jane Kidnie's *The Shakespeare Handbooks: The Taming of the Shrew* (2006), which provides in-depth commentary and information on historical contexts, sources and key productions.

For considering the play in performance, start with *The Taming of the Shrew* in the *Shakespeare in Performance* series (Holderness 1989), which explores various productions of the play on stage and screen. Tori Haring-Smith (1985) focuses on the stage history of the play from the early modern period to the late twentieth century in *From Farce to Metadrama: A Stage History of The Taming of the Shrew, 1594–1983*. For the play on screen see Patricia Lennox's chapter in *The Cambridge Companion to Shakespeare on Screen* (Lennox 2020).

For teachers, a valuable resource is *Approaches to Teaching Shakespeare's The Taming of the Shrew*, edited by Margaret Dupuis and Grace Tiffany, which includes chapters by different writers on the wide range of pedagogical approaches available for teaching the play.

Two contrasting interpretations

Any text is open to contrasting, yet equally valid, interpretations. Here are two different arguments on whether *The Taming of the Shrew* is a feminist play.

Interpretation 1

The Taming of the Shrew is a violent, misogynistic play that assumes the subordination of women is acceptable, and presents a narrative centred on techniques for the subjugation of a woman by her new husband. It follows the trajectory of a feisty and independent woman who is subjected to domestic violence in order to 'tame' and transform her into an obedient wife. Katherina's demonstrations of resistance and autonomy early in the play are quashed and the audience is given the supposed satisfaction of seeing a once outspoken woman being subjugated. As Emily Detmer has argued, the play should be read in the context of theories on domestic violence, conditions such as Stockholm syndrome, and early modern debates on acceptable methods of disciplining wives, which began to favour non-physical methods of control over physical beatings, although without questioning the right of husbands to oppress their wives (Detmer 1997).

That Petruchio does not physically beat Katherina does not make his behaviour less violent. In the contemporary era, his actions would be recognised as coercive control; he isolates Kate from her family, deprives her of food and sleep, and pretends that these acts are a type of kindness. Katherina's right to see her family again depends on her learning to 'see' the world from her husband's perspective and agree with him, regardless of how irrational his statements are. Only by completely submitting to his will and statements can Kate hope to survive in the marriage.

Many of the values endorsed by the play's characters are contrary to contemporary values and pose problems for directors and actors. To present the play as a comedy, as Shakespeare intended, is to risk asking audiences to become complicit in the inherent violence of the play and the process of 'civilising' Katherina and wearing down her spirit of resistance. Rather, the play needs to be recognised as problematic and interpreted without ignoring the unsettling assumptions that lie at its heart.

Interpretation 2

The Taming of the Shrew is a protofeminist play in which Shakespeare challenges the conventional constructions of women of his period. Contrary to early modern assumptions that women should be silent, chaste and obedient, Shakespeare revels in depicting an outspoken woman who defies her family, her society and her suitor. Katherina resists her father's pressure to marry, even though it prevents her younger sister Bianca from marrying, and she asserts her freedom to speak at various points in the play.

Petruchio is quick with language and can match Katherina's insults. Thus, the pair are revealed to be ideally suited. Petruchio, like Kate, is a nonconformist. Whereas other suitors have run from her shrewish behaviour, Petruchio is not dissuaded from his intended course of action. Through the witty arguments between the couple, Shakespeare conveys Katherina's intelligence and education, and the quality of her mind. As Elizabeth Hutcheon argues, the play should be seen in the context of humanist education (an education in classical texts and rhetoric, such as Shakespeare had), according to which Katherina's speech at the end of the play is a display of her ability as a skilled speaker (Hutcheon 2011).

Katherina's contrariness is ultimately displayed when she goes against the expectations of being a shrew and performs the role of obedient wife to enable Petruchio to win a bet. In depicting Katherina as maintaining a resistant stance towards society, Shakespeare presents us with the ultimate feminist. Contrary to the notion that Kate is silenced by her taming, her long, skilled and persuasive speech at the end of the play demonstrates that Kate is unlikely to be silenced in marriage and that, given their matched intelligence and education, the union between Katherina and Petruchio is likely to be a rewarding one. Any notion that Kate's rhetorical speech represents the subordination of a woman also needs to be read in the context of the frame narrative, which implies that the depiction of taming women is a fantasy of the drunkard Sly – an imagined revenge against the hostess who evicted him from the tavern, and as unlikely as the fantasy that he is a lord.

QUESTIONS & ANSWERS

This section focuses on your own analytical writing on the text and gives you strategies for producing high-quality responses in your coursework and exam essays.

Essay writing – an overview

An essay on a literary work is a formal and serious piece of writing that presents your point of view on the text, usually in response to a given topic. Your 'point of view' in an essay is your interpretation of the meaning of the text's language, structure, characters, situations and events, supported by detailed analysis of textual evidence.

Analyse – don't summarise

In your essays it is important to avoid simply summarising what happens in a text.

- A **summary** is a description or paraphrase (retelling in different words) of the characters and events. For example: 'Macbeth has a horrifying vision of a dagger dripping with blood before he goes to murder King Duncan.'
- An **analysis** is an explanation of the real meaning or significance that lies 'beneath' the text's words (and images, for a film). For example: 'Macbeth's vision of a bloody dagger shows how deeply uneasy he is about the violent act he is contemplating and conveys his sense that supernatural forces are impelling him to act.'

A limited amount of summary is sometimes necessary to let your reader know which part of the text you wish to discuss. However, always keep this to a minimum and follow it immediately with your analysis of what this part of the text is really telling us.

Plan your essay

Carefully plan your essay so that you have a clear idea of what you are going to say. The plan ensures that your ideas flow logically, that your argument remains consistent and that you stay on the topic. An essay plan should be a list of **brief dot points** covering no more than half a page.

- Include your central argument or main contention – a concise statement of your overall response to the topic.
- Write three or four dot points for each paragraph indicating the main idea and evidence/examples from the text. Note that in your essay you will need to *expand* on these points and *analyse* the evidence.

Structure your essay

An essay is a complete, self-contained piece of writing. It has a clear beginning (the introduction), middle (several body paragraphs) and end (the last paragraph or conclusion). It must also have a central argument that runs throughout, linking each paragraph to form a coherent whole. See examples of introductions and conclusions in the 'Analysing a sample topic' and 'Sample answer' sections.

The introduction establishes your overall response to the topic. It includes your main contention and outlines the main evidence you will refer to in the course of the essay. Write your introduction *after* you have done a plan and *before* you write the rest of the essay.

The body paragraphs argue your case – they present evidence from the text and explain how this evidence supports your argument. Each body paragraph needs:

- a strong **topic sentence** (usually the first sentence) that states the main point being made in the paragraph
- **evidence** from the text, including some brief quotations
- **analysis** of the textual evidence, with **explanation** of its significance and how it supports your argument
- **links back to the topic** in one or more statements, usually towards the end of the paragraph.

Connect the body paragraphs so that your discussion flows smoothly. Use some linking words and phrases such as 'similarly' and 'on the other hand', though don't start every paragraph like this. Another strategy is to use a significant word from the last sentence of one paragraph in the first sentence of the next.

Use key terms from the topic – or synonyms for them – throughout, so the relevance of your discussion to the topic is always clear.

The conclusion ties everything together and finishes the essay. It includes strong statements that emphasise your central argument and provide a clear response to the topic.

Avoid simply restating the points made earlier in the essay – this will end on a very flat note and imply that you have run out of ideas and vocabulary. The conclusion should be a logical extension of what you have written, not just a repetition or summary of it. Writing an effective conclusion can be a challenge. Try using these tips:

- Start by linking back to the final sentence of the second-last paragraph, rather than leaping back to your main contention straight away – this helps your writing to flow.
- Use synonyms and expressions with equivalent meanings to vary your vocabulary. This allows you to reinforce your line of argument without being repetitive.
- When planning your essay, think of one or two broad statements or observations about the text's wider meaning. These should be related to the topic and your overall argument. Keep them for the conclusion, since they will give you something 'new' to say but still follow logically from your discussion. The introduction will be focused on the topic, but the conclusion can present a wider view of the text.

Essay topics

1. Hortensio: "No mates for you / Unless you were of gentler, milder mould." (1.1.59–60)
   Discuss the construction of gender in *The Taming of the Shrew*.
2. '*The Taming of the Shrew* is one of Shakespeare's most controversial plays.' Discuss.
3. What is the function and significance of the frame narrative in *The Taming of the Shrew*?
4. Explore the motif of disguise in *The Taming of the Shrew*.
5. Analyse the use of insults in *The Taming of the Shrew*. What do they reveal about characters and their relationships?
6. '*The Taming of the Shrew* is a text deeply invested in the idea of education.' (Elizabeth Hutcheon)
   Discuss.
7. How does Shakespeare use language in different ways to convey aspects of the narrative, characters or themes in *The Taming of the Shrew*?
8. Explore the relationship between the two sisters, Katherina and Bianca.
9. Sly: "Am I a lord, and have I such a lady? Or do I dream? Or have I dreamed till now?" (Induction 2.64–5)
   What is the relevance of class in the play? Consider how Shakespeare's historical context informs aspects of the play in this regard.
10. If you were a director, how would you stage *The Taming of the Shrew*? Choose three key scenes and explain how you would stage them and why.

Vocabulary for writing on *The Taming of the Shrew*

Act: major division in a play. In *The Taming of the Shrew* there are five acts, plus the Induction.

Blank verse: plain verse with no rhyming words at the end of the lines; usually in iambic pentameter.

Dramatic irony: when the audience knows something of which a character is unaware.

Early modern: the period from approximately 1500 to 1800.

Elizabethan: the period during which Elizabeth I was on the throne (1558–1603). Plays written after her death in 1603, when James I became king, fall into the Jacobean period.

Foreshadowing: imagery, ideas or events within a literary or dramatic work that anticipate and indicate an event that will occur later in the narrative.

Iambic pentameter: a line of verse with the stresses (beats) falling on every second syllable (the pair of syllables is an iamb); there are five stresses to a line (penta- meaning five), totalling ten syllables.

Medieval: the period roughly from 500 to 1500 (before Shakespeare was writing).

Metadramatic/Metatheatrical: drawing attention to the nature and process of drama and theatre itself.

Metaphor: word or phrase used to describe something else by way of direct comparison. See page 13 in this guide for a discussion of metaphor in *Shrew*.

Oxymoron: contradictory terms used in conjunction (combination).

Personification: figure of speech in which an abstract idea, inanimate object or animal is given human characteristics.

Prose: speech or written language that is plain, not patterned, appearing like ordinary sentences in conversation. The word comes from the Latin word *prosa* meaning 'straightforward discourse'. You will recognise it in the play when the sentences extend to the right margin.

Renaissance: in relation to English literature, the period from the late 1500s up until 1660. Shakespeare wrote in the English Renaissance period.

Scene: subdivision of an act in a play; also describes the physical space in which the action is located on stage. The word 'scene' derives from a Greek word that originally referred to the area behind the stage where the actors would change. Eventually the outside of this structure was decorated to fit in with the performance, leading to the idea of 'scenery'. (Note, however, that very little stage scenery and few props were used in original Shakespearean theatre.)

Simile: similar to a metaphor but using the words 'as' or 'like'. See page 13 in this guide for a discussion of similes in *Shrew*.

Soliloquy: a dramatic speech spoken by a single character, usually when alone on stage.

Stage direction: note in the text of a play that tells actors what to do. These are generally minimal in plays from the Elizabethan and Jacobean periods.

Verse: a line of metrical writing. The word 'meter' comes from the Greek word for 'measure' and refers to a pattern of stressed and unstressed syllables. You can often identify verse in a play when you see that a character's speech lines don't extend to the right margin. In Shakespeare's plays the verse is in iambic pentameter and often uses rhyme. (The word 'verse' can also refer to a stanza, which is a paragraph in a poem, and to poetry in general.)

Analysing a sample topic

Explore the motif of disguise in *The Taming of the Shrew*.

There are various ways you could approach this topic. In the play, disguise is used for different aims and effects so you could focus on one of these in depth, or choose to analyse several different aspects, as this sample outline does. Consider whether there is a connecting element in the various ways that disguise is used in the play, and draw on that to draft your statement of argument for the introduction.

Sample introduction

> Disguise is a key motif in William Shakespeare's *The Taming of the Shrew* (1590–91), and is used to create various effects and for different dramatic purposes. This essay will consider three key aspects of disguise: comic effect, focusing on the frame narrative and Bianca's suitors; class, exploring the implications of Tranio disguising himself as Lucentio; and gender roles, exploring the behaviour of Katherina and Petruchio. I argue that through the motif of disguise in the play, Shakespeare demonstrates that role-playing is central to human interactions and behaviour.

Body paragraph outline

Body paragraph 1

Topic sentence: Disguise is a key method of creating comic effect in the play.

- It would be useful to start with the frame narrative: the Lord plays a trick on Sly, and the page Bartholomew disguises himself as Sly's wife. How is the comic effect created here?
- You could then explore the comedy of wooing Bianca, noting why the various suitors have to disguise themselves (i.e. discuss Bianca's →

father not allowing her to marry before her older sister Katherina, meaning the various suitors have to devise ways to get closer to Bianca). Find examples and some representative quotations from the play to set the scene. Then analyse some of the comic moments that are created by the suitors being in disguise.

- You could also discuss **dramatic irony** – several of the comic effects are created due to Baptista being unaware that the scholars he has hired to instruct Bianca are in fact attempting to instruct her in the art of love.
- Then you could conclude with some observations on Lucentio's disguise and how it is successful in wooing Bianca. This would allow for a **linking sentence** to the next paragraph, which looks at the effects of Tranio impersonating Lucentio.

Body paragraph 2

Topic sentence: The impersonation of Lucentio by Tranio challenges class hierarchies while also creating dramatic interest.

- In this paragraph it would be useful to begin with historical context on the hierarchical nature of Shakespeare's society. Not only was rank strictly observed, it was indicated by different types of clothing.
- Outline why Lucentio has Tranio impersonate him and how Tranio is shown to be intelligent in competing successfully for Bianca on behalf of his master.
- Consider the dramatic interest created by the challenge of Tranio having to make good on his promise and produce 'Vincentio', played by a merchant in disguise.
- Conclude the paragraph with a linking sentence that segues to your next topic, perhaps by questioning whether gender roles could also be seen as a type of disguise.

Body paragraph 3

Topic sentence: Both Katherina and Petruchio behave in ways that challenge their society's expectations about gender roles, masking their underlying feelings and motivations through playing certain roles.

- Broaden the topic of disguise into gender roles. How does Kate play the shrew when we first meet her in the play and what are the reasons she behaves as she does?
- Then think about the final scene where Kate chooses to play the role of submissive wife; discuss why she might do this.
- You could explore how Petruchio also defies society expectations. For example, his ridiculous outfit at the wedding is a type of disguise – what are his motivations? Is Petruchio's behaviour as an irrational and cruel husband also a type of disguise and, if so, to what effect?
- Conclude with your thoughts on the effect of the two lead characters' behaviour and role-playing.

Sample conclusion

Disguise is a key motif in the play, used in various ways. Shakespeare creates comedy through the various suitors adopting disguises to gain access to Bianca, implying that, in wooing, lovers are always adopting and playing a role. The inversion of class status when Tranio disguises himself as Lucentio and successfully obtains Bianca for his master implicitly questions society's rigid hierarchical rankings, showing that a witty and intelligent servant is capable of playing the role of his superiors. Furthermore, the shrewish behaviour of Katherina and Petruchio can be read as a type of role-playing, a disguise for underlying emotions and motivations. Ultimately, the motif of disguise in Shakespeare's play suggests that role-playing is central to human motivations and behaviour.

SAMPLE ANSWER

Discuss the construction of gender in *The Taming of the Shrew.*

William Shakespeare's *The Taming of the Shrew* (1590–91) is a controversial play that raises a range of questions for a contemporary audience about the construction of gender and roles in marriage. In this essay, I will firstly outline some of the historical contexts relevant to the play, then examine aspects of gender and violence before considering how the character of Katherina challenges the gendered expectations of the period. I argue that while the play needs to be read in the context of early modern assumptions about gender, Shakespeare leaves room for interpretations of the play that accord with contemporary values.

In the early modern period, women were thought of as a type of property that belonged firstly to their fathers and then to their husbands. They generally did not own property themselves; instead, they *were* property. Petruchio expresses this idea after the wedding when he states 'She is my goods, my chattels', but then goes on to comically exaggerate this idea in 'she is my house, / My household-stuff, my field, my barn, / My horse, my ox, my ass, my anything' (3.2.219–21). Furthermore, because women were treated as objects rather than subjects, they were usually denied the opportunity for an education. Widows often generated anxiety as they could be more autonomous than wives; Hortensio's attitude towards his new wife needs to be interpreted in this context, especially when he expresses the idea that Petruchio is educating him in how to tame an outspoken woman (4.5.78–9). While this is comic from one perspective, the notion of taming also implies violence.

Violence comes in various forms in the play. The first type of violence is inherent in the assumption that Katherina and Bianca are types of property: objects rather than subjects with their own agency. Katherina is characterised as old, unwanted stock – to be sold 'with all faults' (1.1.124), a phrase from the cattle market – while Bianca, a 'jewel' (1.2.113), is more valuable. Bianca is treated like an item at an auction, sold to the highest bidder in 2.1. The treatment of daughters as possessions to be transferred to husbands led to the potential for violence in the home, where women were subject to the will of their husbands. Although the scene after Katherina and Petruchio's wedding is intended to be comic, the idea of a wife being denied food and sleep is disturbing.

Women at this time were expected to be chaste, silent and obedient, and it is the expectation of silence that the figure of the shrew particularly challenges. The shrew was outspoken and used language to challenge men's claim to dominance; this is encapsulated in the figure of Katherina. Kate powerfully articulates the right of women to speak, at a time when women were expected to be silent. In 4.3, having been deprived of food and sleep, Katherina asserts:

> Why, sir, I trust I may have leave to speak,
> And speak I will. I am no child, no babe.
> Your betters have endured me say my mind,
> And if you cannot, best you stop your ears.
> My tongue will tell the anger of my heart,
> Or else my heart concealing it will break,
> And, rather than it shall, I will be free
> Even to the uttermost, as I please, in words. (4.3.73–80)

Here Katherina claims a freedom to speak and Shakespeare, in creating such a powerful female character, gives voice to these ideas of resistance. The treatment of women as property owned by their husbands was not only harmful to women but also to men, since it denied them the opportunity to develop marital relationships based on equality and a meeting of minds. Shakespeare's recognition of this need for greater equality and mutual respect is implicit in his depiction of the main characters.

A key idea in the early modern period was that of the golden mean: that moderation is the key to life. Katherina's behaviour at the beginning of the play, and Petruchio's after the wedding, represent extremes of behaviour. Both Katherina and Petruchio are verbally and physically violent. However, the two extremes come together and reach a state of moderation at the end of the play. Furthermore, while the subject of Katherina's last speech is wifely obedience, the form of the speech, as a highly skilled, rhetorical performance, is in fact giving Kate a voice and resisting the idea that women are not entitled to an education or a voice in public life. While there are limits to the play's protofeminism, due to its early modern context, the marriage between Kate and Petruchio has the potential for a mutually rewarding intellectual bond in which each respects the other.

REFERENCES & READING

Text

Brady, L (ed.) 2014, *The Taming of the Shrew*, Cambridge University Press, Cambridge. All quotations and most of the 'key vocabulary' definitions have been drawn from this edition.

References

Ackroyd, P 2005, *Shakespeare: The Biography*, Vintage, London.

Bate, J 1997, *The Genius of Shakespeare*, Picador, London.

—— 2008, *Soul of the Age*, Penguin, London.

De Grazia, M & Wells, S (eds) 2010, *The New Cambridge Companion to Shakespeare*, 2nd edn, Cambridge University Press, Cambridge.

Detmer, E 1997, 'Civilising Subordination: Domestic Violence and *The Taming of the Shrew*', *Shakespeare Quarterly*, vol. 48, pp.273–94.

Dobson, M, Wells, S, Sharpe, W & Sullivan, E (eds) 2015, *The Oxford Companion to Shakespeare*, 2nd edn, Oxford University Press, Oxford.

Driver, E, Forbes, S, Mapps, J & Trewby, M (eds) 2009, *The Shakespeare Encyclopedia*, Global Book Publishing, Sydney.

Dupuis, M & Tiffany, G (eds) 2013, *Approaches to Teaching Shakespeare's The Taming of the Shrew*, The Modern Language Association of America, New York.

Garber, M 2004, *Shakespeare After All*, Anchor Books, New York.

Gay, P 2008, *The Cambridge Introduction to Shakespeare's Comedies*, Cambridge University Press, Cambridge.

Greenblatt, S 2004, *Will in the World: How Shakespeare Became Shakespeare*, Pimlico, London.

Haring-Smith, T 1985, *From Farce to Metadrama: A Stage History of The Taming of the Shrew, 1594–1983*, Greenwood Press, London.

Holderness, G 1989, *The Taming of the Shrew*, Manchester University Press, Manchester.

Howard, JE 2016, Introduction to *The Taming of the Shrew* in S Greenblatt, S Gossett, W Cohen, JE Howard, KE Maus & G McMullen (eds), *The Norton Shakespeare*, WW Norton & Company, New York.

Hutcheon, E 2011, 'From Shrew to Subject: Petruchio's Humanist Education of Katherine in *The Taming of the Shrew*', *Comparative Drama*, vol. 45, no. 4, pp.315–37.

Kermode, F 2001, *Shakespeare's Language*, Penguin, London.

Kidnie, MJ 2006, *The Shakespeare Handbooks: The Taming of the Shrew*, Palgrave Macmillan, New York.

Leggatt, A (ed.) 2001, *The Cambridge Companion to Shakespearean Comedy*, Cambridge University Press, Cambridge.

Lennox, P 2020, 'Violence, Tragic and Comic, in *Coriolanus* and *The Taming of the Shrew*' in R Jackson (ed.), *The Cambridge Companion to Shakespeare on Screen*, Cambridge University Press, Cambridge, pp.173–86.

Films

The Taming of the Shrew 1967, dir. Franco Zeffirelli, Columbia Pictures. Starring Elizabeth Taylor and Richard Burton.

The Taming of the Shrew 1980, dir. Jonathan Miller, BBC Television. Starring John Cleese and Sarah Badel.

10 Things I Hate About You 1999, dir. Gil Junger, Touchstone Pictures, Mad Chance and Jaret Entertainment. Starring Julia Stiles and Heath Ledger.

Musical

Kiss Me, Kate 1948, written by Bella Spewack and Samuel Spewack. Music and lyrics by Cole Porter.

Websites

British Library, www.bl.uk/works/the-taming-of-the-shrew

Folger Shakespeare Library, www.folger.edu/taming-of-the-shrew

Shakespeare Birthplace Trust, www.shakespeare.org.uk/